Y0-CAE-505

SONATA

Also by Charles Bowden

Killing the Hidden Waters (1977)

Street Signs Chicago: Neighborhood and Other Illusions of Big-City Life, with Lewis Kreinberg and Richard Younker (1981)

Blue Desert (1986)

Frog Mountain Blues, with Jack W. Dykinga (1987)

Trust Me: Charles Keating and the Missing Billions, with Michael Binstein (1988)

Mezcal (1988)

Red Line (1989)

Desierto: Memories of the Future (1991)

The Sonoran Desert, with Jack W. Dykinga (1992)

The Secret Forest, with Jack W. Dykinga and Paul S. Martin (1993)

Blood Orchid: An Unnatural History of America (1995)

Chihuahua: Pictures From the Edge, with Virgil Hancock (1996)

Stone Canyons of the Colorado Plateau, with Jack W. Dykinga (1996)

Juárez: The Laboratory of Our Future, with Noam Chomsky, Eduardo Galeano, and Julián Cardona (1998)

Eugene Richards, with Eugene Richards (2001)

Down by the River: Drugs, Money, Murder, and Family (2002)

Blues for Cannibals: The Notes from Underground (2002)

A Shadow in the City: Confessions of an Undercover Drug Warrior (2005)

Inferno, with Michael P. Berman (2006)

Exodus/Éxodo, with Julián Cardona (2008)

Some of the Dead Are Still Breathing: Living in the Future (2009)

Trinity, with Michael P. Berman (2009)

Murder City: Ciudad Juárez and the Global Economy's New Killing Fields, with Julián Cardona (2010)

Dreamland: The Way Out of Juárez, with Alice Leora Briggs (2010)

The Charles Bowden Reader, edited by Erin Almeranti and Mary Martha Miles (2010)

El Sicario: The Autobiography of a Mexican Assassin, with Molly Molloy (2011)

The Red Caddy: Into the Unknown with Edward Abbey (2018)

Dakotah: The Return of the Future (2019)

Jericho (2020)

SONATA

Charles Bowden

FOREWORD BY
ALFREDO CORCHADO

University of Texas Press
Austin

Printed in the United States of America
First edition, 2020

♾ The paper used in this book meets the minimum requirements of ANSI/NISO Z39.48-1992 (R1997) (Permanence of Paper).
Library of Congress Cataloging-in-Publication Data

Names: Bowden, Charles, 1945-2014, author.
Title: Sonata / Charles Bowden ; foreword by Alfredo Corchado.
Description: First edition. | Austin : University of Texas Press, 2020. | Includes bibliographical references.
Identifiers: LCCN 2020018410 (print) | LCCN 2020018411 (ebook)
ISBN 978-1-4773-2223-9 (hardcover)
ISBN 978-1-4773-2224-6 (ebook other)
ISBN 978-1-4773-2225-3 (ebook)
Subjects: LCSH: Bowden, Charles, 1945-2014—Homes and haunts. | Immigrants—Mexican-American Border Region—Social conditions. | Drug control—Social aspects—Mexican-American Border Region. | Border crossing—Social aspects—Mexican-American Border Region. | Nature and civilization—Mexican-American Border Region. | Nature, Healing power of. | Mexican-American Border Region—Social conditions. | LCGFT: Creative nonfiction.
Classification: LCC PS3552.O844 S66 2020 (print) | LCC PS3552.O844 (ebook) | DDC 814/.54—dc23
LC record available at https://lccn.loc.gov/2020018410
LC ebook record available at https://lccn.loc.gov/2020018411

doi:10.7560/322239

Fronterizos

ALFREDO CORCHADO

America again is afire and I can't help but think of Charles Bowden. Years after his death, his striking, adversarial, dark voice from the border is notably absent in these times of seething outrage.

A native of the Midwest and a veteran chronicler of human misery and tragedy, Bowden found his calling on the US-Mexico border. This is clearly underscored by his last work, *Sonata*, one of the unpublished manuscripts found on his computer after he died in August 2014. *Sonata*, finished a month before he died, is the last of six books that he intended as parts of a series titled "An Unnatural History of America."

To me and others rooted here, the border is simply the place we call home. But in US popular culture—including country songs, western movies, countless novels, and travel pieces—the border is too often painted as a raw, untamed place that offers escape from America's disappointments or often stultifying abundance. A magnet for exiles seeking a safe haven from a preordained destiny, the border is more than geography. It's also a mindset, a homeland for the constant parade of pilgrims and desperados driven by a quest for renewal.

Some of them, depicting my homeland, do so from a place of privilege. Plenty of others have brought empathy and humility, offering to borderland natives with fresh eyes and wandering hearts a cry for justice, a plea to the better angels inside us. Somehow, divergent worlds blur or widen, depending on the prism of the baggage we carry.

For some stalwart reporters, like John Reed, it was a place to come of age, as the Oregonian rode with Pancho Villa in *Insurgent Mexico*. For others, including many midwesterners I've had the honor of knowing, the border never quite surrenders its beguiling, firm embrace.

Some are hell-bent on raising uncomfortable truths, pushing back against conventional talking points. Bowden was one of that kind.

Sonata, as the last and, perhaps surprisingly, most hopeful piece of the sextet serves as part of his epitaph.

Which is not to say that Bowden has given up making readers uncomfortable. "There comes a season when the hungry dogs want to be fed. I realize I have died far too early and must return. I crave flesh, sun and stars," Bowden writes in the book's opening lines. *Sonata*'s meandering ride doesn't get any smoother after that.

If you open the book expecting to read *Down by the River*, Bowden's much-acclaimed work in which he weaves a gripping tale of treachery, deceit, corruption, and death on both sides of the US-Mexico border, *stop. Sonata* is not a linear narrative.

At times, Bowden's writing in *Sonata* feels like stream of consciousness. One passage is set on his cousin's farm in Iowa; another is about Vincent van Gogh. He writes about a black door, a borderless heron, and Mexico's seemingly endless drug war complicated by what he views as the globalization's plague.

"Miles run all over my face," Bowden writes here. "I have traveled back to where I began on a farm by a creek with fish jumping and just down the hills the big stacks at the mills filling the blue sky with smoke.

"All the miles behind me, all those dead ends and closing time drinks and women, that is some other season before I left," he reflects about a return visit to the US heartland that is no longer home to him. "Now I am that man without a country or a flag. You cross the line, you become a traitor."

Then there's the furor over a border wall that grew as a menacing scar under the Bush and Obama administrations before becoming a daily obsession.

"There is a wall and it is patrolled by the questions we ask and the words we choose," he writes in *Sonata*, reawakening a deepening wound that would only grow more painful in the Trump era.

Bowden's love of the untamed might have drawn him closer to the border. He waxed poetically about "the line," a two-thousand-mile frontier, yet was not afraid to tell the truth about Juárez's murdered women. Bodies strewn across a vast desert. As one wired for optimism, I find many of his writings at times jarring, in their descriptions of my home as apocalyptic, an inferno-bound runaway train.

He wasn't entirely off.

I first heard of Bowden's work in 1998 with the book *Juárez: The Laboratory of Our Future*. I devoured the book, as it challenged my more sanguine view of the hardscrabble city that has been my family's second home since I first arrived at the age of five.

I came face-to-face with Juaritos, as I fondly refer to the city, in 1965. Construction was booming. Homes built of cinder block, sheets of aluminum, plywood, and even cardboard, blooming in the blazing desert summer and hunkering down in the bitterly cold winters. The city's rich, then and now, living behind high walls, with the poor relegated to the barren hills that sprawl across the narrow Rio Grande stream, up against the looming shadow of the University of Texas at El Paso, UTEP—my alma mater.

Up to fifty thousand Mexicans a year, including my family

and I, were arriving in Ciudad Juárez eager to fill jobs created by the mostly US-owned factories known as maquiladoras. This was right after the Bracero guest worker program ended, leaving millions who once worked in farm fields and meatpacking plants jobless.

My family hails from San Luis de Cordero in rural Durango, a village embraced by mountains whose beauty is only marred by a suffocating drought. Soon enough, uncles, aunts, and cousins became dependent on the border's slave wages, for they were better than what we left behind. We came because we were told we had a chance. Aunt Carmelina built a house near hills later covered with giant letters for all to see: "La Biblia Es La Verdad. Leela. *The Bible Is Truth. Read It*."

We all waited for an opening to a better life, cursed by the promise of the First World.

Raw and desperate, Juárez still offered hope.

But there was something wrong about all this growth. The city swelled from some 350,000 in 1965 to about 1.4 million today, yet its leaders somehow conveniently ignored the need to accommodate the newcomers. Not enough schools, parks, or housing for the workers and their families. Too many dirt streets without names remained unpaved, and the few schools were a joke.

Juárez was a sprawl of concrete under a scorching sun sitting not quite like an oasis in the desert, yet enough to beckon Mexicans from all regions. People's dreams and hopes simply overwhelmed the city. Then, in the mid-1980s, a whiff of change lured both young and old into the streets to demand more locally generated wealth for their city from the national coffers in Mexico City. Unrest and jubilation. As a young reporter for the *El Paso Herald-Post*, I followed the cries for justice, walking alongside protesters, notepad in my hand, witnessing history, recording a thirst for democracy.

The spark that began here at the turn of the century brought alternate governments to Mexico, with the ballot-box ouster of the Institutional Revolutionary Party, or PRI, which had ruled Mexico with an iron fist since 1929.

And as the PRI's power dissipated, its semiauthoritarian government loosened its grip and the narco boys, once semi-disciplined, grew wild. The dam broke. That was my vision of Juárez, warts and all.

Bowden saw the promise in Juárez but described it also as ripe for imperialist aims, a reservoir for violence and desperate migrants. Now, the more I read Bowden, the more I wish I had known him better. His stories today are just as relevant as when he wrote them—if not more so. He wrote about the maquila industry and the definition of who and what is an essential worker (before the term became trendy), from those toiling in the assembly lines to top supervisors with private health insurance. Death knows no class or status, as many died of COVID-19 in 2020 as the Mexican government downplayed the death toll and the US government, led by its ambassador in Mexico City, waged a campaign with corporate America to get everyone back to work and save the global supply at the expense of lives. I thought of an incensed Bowden. His rage.

We met at least twice, briefly and superficially.

One afternoon, freelance photographer Christ Chavez, who knew Bowden, was on assignment with me. We were reporting on a story that I had broken earlier about a gruesome find: bodies buried in the backyard of a house in a middle-class neighborhood of Juárez, with rows of other homes. Bowden, in a subsequent book, referred to it as "The House of Death."

This was a story about narcos, informants, and their US handlers and the deadly consequences. The madness was orchestrated by someone who even recommended the best way to dispatch victims, either with a gun or by suffocation with plastic bags to keep the noise down.

A man named Lalo held the keys to the house, where drug

dealers were executed by corrupt police officers on Lalo's orders. Lalo was also a paid American informant for the US Immigration and Customs Enforcement agency, or ICE. This obviously made the story that much more intriguing and relevant to a US audience.

Of course, Americans were hungry for such grisly stories reinforcing their view of Mexicans as bloodthirsty. I was there feeding them daily. Other foreign press members, too, swarmed to the border, parking their rented vehicles outside that House of Death. Bowden was front row. Complicating things: we shared a key source, Phil Jordan, a former DEA agent who was featured prominently in Bowden's *Down by the River*.

Jordan fed us material and alerted me of "Chuck's" next step. I'm sure he did the same with Bowden, a timeless tactic by spooks: keep competitive reporters darting, anxious for the next bone.

"I ask the agent about the dead coming out of the patio of a home across the river," Bowden writes in *Sonata*, refreshing old memories of Jordan. "He shrugs and says they are all bad people, who cares? Maybe that is when I begin to leave. Or maybe that is when I should have left."

Christ returned from taking pictures of the House of Death with a smirk. He sarcastically quipped: "Your hero is over there." He meant Bowden. He's asking, Christ said, why he never sees you around. My pride was wounded. As we drove by the house I glimpsed Bowden's longish, thinning blond hair and lanky frame and confess I felt conflicted: Was he a hero of the working class—yet another white knight coming to rescue us—or just healthy competition?

I saw Bowden a second time, at an event in El Paso, and this time I mustered the courage to say hi. He looked at me, sized me up, and with a sly, wide grin blurted in his cantankerous, gravelly voice: "I'm surprised we haven't met before."

"I try keeping a low profile," I replied and added, "They're killing reporters out there. I'm American, even have a US passport, but I still look Mexican."

We stared at each other for a second, maybe two, then we went our separate ways.

Regrettably, those would be my last words to him. I would never see Bowden again.

These days, America looks unhinged: Protesters march through streets across the country. In El Paso one handwritten sign reads: "Silence is violence." And the ubiquitous "Sin Justicia, No Hay Paz." "No Justice, No Peace."

It feels like a watershed moment, like so many others I continue to witness in Mexico. I returned to Bowden's *Sonata* for answers, for reflection, and found comfort in the unvarnished, hardened truth. Bowden came to write about the border and like so many before him left a part of himself here in this land of misfits, as the outside world often views us. He became a *fronterizo*, carrying with him battle scars from previous wars but offering much-needed context for today's troubled times.

Scars, of course, are healed wounds. Their visibility is a reminder of both the pain and that it can be healed. In this they are hopeful, and, fittingly for the ultimate book in this series, that spirit animates *Sonata*: "He looks up and feels dread. He looks up and feels hope. Van Gogh goes back and forth on what he finds in the night sky." So it was with my family in 1965, the protestors of 1980s Juárez, and the protestors of today.

"'There can be no beauty without accepting the people behind the black metal door. Just as I long ago learned that there can be no justice without heeding the man who wants to know which way is Atlanta," Bowden movingly wrote. "And there can be no peace without cranes in the sky and dancing in the marshes."

As I finish the last pages of Bowden's *Sonata*, I feel the urge to write, again.

SONATA

PART I
Love among the Bloods

They grope in the darkness without light, and he maketh them to stagger like a drunken man.

JOB 12:25

There comes a season when the hungry dogs want to be fed. I realize I have died far too early and must return. I crave flesh, sun and stars.

In a café, an agent leans on the blond Formica-topped table. The floor red with Saltillo tile. The walls prints of idyllic Mexico, a woman in a blue rebozo, a child with flowers, clay images of the sun, and on the walls it is always morning in a fresh world.

I ask the agent about the dead coming out of the patio of a home across the river.

He shrugs and says they are all bad people, who cares?

Maybe that is when I begin to leave.

Or maybe that is when I should have left.

I listen to the water, a green tongue of effluent spewing from the sewage plant. The violated stream is all that is left of a big river after the hungers of the cities and farms.

Crows talk over the weak light of winter. The river is now green-winged teal, northern shovelers, mallards. A belted kingfisher hunts from the power line and redtail hawks from the north crowd in. The Cooper's hawk moves through the bosques, kestrels lurk in the bare cottonwoods.

I can hear cranes somewhere out of sight in a field.

I cling to these moments, pieces of gold in a gale of counterfeit currencies.

Upstream a dead sandhill crane lies in the field, black-tipped wings arcing to the blue sky. A flotilla of common mergansers ride on the pond, geese honk overhead. I mutter the names like beads on some rosary. A front is moving in, the air is warm but the sky fills with warnings.

Mother

Having stopped being afraid, I stopped brooding and started rediscovering the world. I started seeing trees again, the children in the streets, the poor laboring in the fields. . . .

Mothers called their children from the windows. It was a time favorable to Humility. Man returned to the animal, the animal to the plant, the plant to the earth. The stream at the bottom of the valley was full of stars.

IGNAZIO SILONE, *Bread and Wine*

The music never died but at times I wondered about me. In the morning light, I hear the upright piano in the big room. Outside, there is the clucking of chickens and cattle low in the meadows. It is always spring save a few days when snow falls and the flakes cling to my memory. For the rest, spring with fresh breezes, seedlings popping up in the garden, a rank odor from the leaves of the tomatoes brushing against my fingers.

Sap flows from my mother's arm, her head is leaves, eyes blue corn flowers, her lips of plum tomatoes open and she says, "You will never wander from the dirt in this garden, you are of the blood with the night crawlers, the weasel sneaking into the hen house, the hawk in the sky."

She never said this and that is why I always remember it.

She fed bums that came to the back door. They would sit on the stoop and eat their plate clean.

She harbored the illegals, too.

Then the wind came up and I lost it all for a spell.

Now they work out back. My mother is dead. The sky blue.

The small child squeals with delight as he harvests fallen nuts on the winter ground. His father stares straight ahead—damage to an eye means pain if he bends down. The wife works beside him. They cannot go back, the killings stop them, and if they go back, they will die. There is no question about that fact.

A crow squawks.

The leafless trees stir with hints of sap.

Rasputin, before the women, before the drinking, before the Czarina, before the cold death in the Neva, back when Rasputin is a boy, this he remembers: "When I was fifteen, in my village, in the summertime, when the sun shone warmly and the birds sang heavenly songs, I walked along the path and did not dare go along the middle of it. I was dreaming about God. My soul was longing to fly afar. I often wept and did not know where the tears came from and what they were for."

The child cries out with delight and the half-blind man harvests pecans from the ground but he never bends.

I reach out to catch a bird on the wing, feathers ruffle my fingers, and the blood rises drowning good intentions with the tongues of hell.

Nijinsky studies the dance in the capital. He gets lucky and wins 500 rubles at the tables. Each day he'd pass streetwalkers looking lean along the river. He takes six to a dinner. They devour the food, throw down the wine. Nijinsky is horrified, pitches his money on the table and leaves. The madness comes later when he has gone so far into the dance no one has ever been able to follow him.

I am walking down a dirt lane. I can't shake these things. Rasputin prattles about God, Nijinsky takes whores to dinner and recoils from the face of hunger.

The light is leaving. My mind is empty of thoughts and I am nothing but appetites. A man slides out of the tall grass with that look of the hunted. I pretend he is not there. I fail.

He also devours the food. But he does not touch the wine.

And I do not leave.

Crossing the Line

If we let ourselves be guided by the atonal musician we walk as it were through a dense forest. The strangest flowers and plants attract our attention by the side of the path. But we do not know where we are going nor whence we have come. The listener is seized by a feeling of being lost, of being at the mercy of the forces of primeval existence.

WILHELM FURTWANGLER

Come morning, bees hover over the lavender bloom of the deadly nightshade as night slowly gives up on the valley. Sycamores shadow the creek crossing where the raven pays me no never mind. It is sixty feet, then thirty, then twenty feet away. The bird eyes me, then bends that powerful neck and goes back to hunting the stream. I've been feeding a pair scraps of meat each morning. When this one does not bolt, I feel accepted, an unusual sensation for me. Light splashes the ground as the sun pokes through the cottonwoods. The chill of the night lingers in the shadows. A red-tailed nestling sits upright on a bare limb, the head covered with a light down. Then a thick-billed kingbird lands on a dead limb. I trust these moments more than money.

He comes over from time to time. This begins before the zone-tailed hawks know my face. He's always friendly and he always asks questions. Some people call him a sneak because of his questions, a guy snooping around trying to catch people. I remember once telling him that I'd meet him in a local café. He hesitated and then said he didn't think he should go there. Later, a bunch of local people went down, including the ones running the café. That bust flattened the economy of patches of the town.

He works intelligence for the agency, interviews wayfarers plucked from the daily catch. He's been obsessed with one smuggler for over ten years.

The guy hardly ever crosses, always uses others as puppets and then sits across the line pulling strings. Once he'd met the guy right on the line and they'd stood there facing each other across the fence. This was back in the day before the walls, even before the car barriers, back when the border was a line and five-strand barbed wire to keep the stock from drifting.

The guy said, "I'm crossing fifty Brazilians tomorrow, right along this stretch and you can't stop me."

There was a time the guy was picked up with a group of illegals but nobody would finger him as a smuggler and so eventually he was let go as just another migrant flung back across the line.

The agent pauses here in his telling, he kind of leans back and stares off into the creek. Two gray hawks scream and then vanish into the top of a cottonwood. It's the time of nesting. His eyes catch them but he hangs onto his story.

He says, "And by God, he did it, right under our noses. He did it for years."

He leans back in the metal chair the green paint now fading.

One time I asked how many of the people he trusted at work.

He fell silent.

Finally, he said, "No one."

Those were the good times, the simple times, before it all got too hopeless, those times back when he was hunting that guy who dared him with his boast of moving fifty Brazilians right under his nose. Now something has changed for him. He can still do the job—the pay's good and the pension beckons at the end of that corridor of years.

Back then, the zone-tailed hawks did not brush against my life and I was ignorant of their cries in the forest. And he could still do his job without a qualm.

The Tall Grass

Now my life lies around me like bones whitening on the ground under an empty sky. The bones once held a body together before the big killing came but now that body must be imagined if the bones are ever going to be reassembled as a skeleton that can hold flesh. There is the love of spring, the need to help people, the lust for the flesh, the cries of the hawks, purr of water on a streambed and the downy head of the young raptor peering out over the nest of twigs with fresh eyes. There is the moment when a man slides out of the tall grass and he is hungry and his hunger is against the laws.

Since my childhood I have felt a life that was whole but in the telling it always became broken dreams and pieces of glass bottles gleaming in the alley—the sunrise, the job, her scent on the pillow, the slow flap of wings as a heron passed, and in the telling everything came out faint and little bits and lacking substance. I feel a shadow pass the face of the moon. I find the same shattered feeling in newspapers, books, talk in the cafés, voices in the whiskey bars.

There is a song in our heads, one we learned when our mothers carried us, and yet we lose the tune and there comes a day when our singing wounds the sky and fills our own ears with horror and yet we know the song is still there, just beyond our ability or maybe just past our courage, no matter, the song becomes a mutilated thing, a chord here, a smattering of notes on faded parchment there, ink fading and the key is increasingly hard to make out. The keyboard has broken off the harpsichord, the shattered shell of a lute, the golden saxophone with a dented body, the slender dream of the clarinet clogged with mud, all this, and I can hear the tune faintly and feel the notes but when I come to say the song it shreds or breaks or loses its structure.

I walk to the gate and in the gray light clouds scud on the surface of a mud puddle and then, the clouds part, light suddenly bounces off the puddle into my eye, I start, an Inca dove flutters up, and in the tangle of the bank the blue throat of a morning glory glows among the green. A bird calls, four Mexican vultures sit on a pole and I hear a voice and she speaks and the borders in my mind vanish. I can hear her and just now I look up and see a bobcat ambling across the red brick patio in front of the French doors but it pays me no mind though it knows I am standing here and I say not a word as it slowly walks down the slope and disappears into the coyote willows and she knocks at the door. There was a time in another house when she comes in without a hello clutching a big bottle of wine and pours some and starts talking, her face serious, a touch of sad there lingering around her inviting lips and she says, "Can I ever be any good at this, I mean what do you think?" and she goes on like that, the wine, the question, for hours and she keeps getting calls from the guy she lives with—"I find used condoms and he never uses them with me so what do you think that means?"—and I feel things slipping, the edges washing away, the lines erased, the boundaries they tell of in school gone for good, and she drinks and talks and she keeps using the bathroom and never closes the door and at one point I go to a table and write something down and when I turn in my chair she is standing there with her blouse off and a wine glass in one hand and outside the storm gathers, the birds are greedy at the feeders, they know, they can feel the blow coming sweeping down the valley, and she asks, "Am I any good or am I just wasting my time doing this?" and I avoid the question because I don't want to hand out defeat or awards, because her face is all want and I cannot fill that want, there is some line.

Bones, stars wheeling overhead, her sad eyes, the scent off her breasts, her need to matter, to do something well, the fear in her eyes that life is slipping through her fingers, a hunger for dawn and fresh loves, a hunger for the act, for doing the right thing and no longer caring about the judgment days that howl on the mountain, and she wants what I want then and want now, to go out the door and find real work on real ground and avoid the laws that can't make sense of spring flowers or love or death.

She is part of the bones whitening on the floor of my mind, the shards and scraps that for me are the whole, the snatches of life that connect but refuse to surrender to a theory or doom or a solution.

And finally I walk her out and put her in her car and she rolls down the window and says she wants to spend two days in a motel and then the night takes her and her hungry heart away.

Hush

The story goes like this: the retired military guy learns one of his relatives has been kidnapped. So he calls up another officer, one he trained and mentored. He explains the problem.

The guy he calls, well, he heads the security for the president of Mexico and spends his time in the heart of things at Los Pinos, the presidential mansion in Mexico City. The man takes care of it, the kidnappers release the victim unharmed.

The retired officer knew it would all go well, after all he trained up the guy.

He knows it will be clean, no trace of whatever happened or did not happen, no trace at all.

Clean.

The way things should be.

The story goes like this: the pharmacist is kidnapped and they want a lot of money. He is beaten hard and so is another captive, a young guy.

After one beating the young guy says, "I am not going to make it. When you are released tell my father I love him."

The family comes up with the hundred thousand and the pharmacist is dumped on the street. Two or three days later, he hobbles to the place where the father of the young man lives. He tells him he brings a message from his son. The father says the family buried him two days ago. They could not come up with the money.

The pharmacist delivers the message.

The father weeps.

What strikes me is I hear the first story in the cool of a June morning with bird song in the trees. And I hear the second story in a house in a barrio and it is over a hundred outside and there is one fan moving air inside. And both times I feel very cold, and my bones are ice.

The air is still, voices drift in from the street. Sheets cover the shelves to hold back the dust. The plants struggle in the garden. The beans do not produce well, the tomatoes suffer.

I hear the word hush.

You cannot write this, you cannot repeat this.

Hush.

It could put lives at stake.

Hush.

It is not positive.

Hush.

And little of it will be recorded and little that is recorded will be remembered and almost none of it is even mentioned now.

The blood dries, the tears stop falling.

It never happened.

Hush.

The Asylum

She is crazy. She is pretty, baby. Sometimes she leaves the asylum and wanders the streets. Sometimes her son visits her in the asylum with his wife and child. She loves them and they love her but she cannot live with them because these moments come. She cannot stop such moments.

She meets a man she knew long ago before she became crazy and before she moved into the asylum. They fall in love all over again. They will be married. The man running the asylum plans to spend hundreds of dollars he does not have for the wedding, the dress, the fiesta. He thinks it will be good for the other crazy people who live in the desert in the asylum.

But then she just keels over and dies. There is no explanation. There is no money for answers.

They bury her in her wedding dress.

The air sags with wood smoke at the asylum, the dogs are hungry and at night they howl.

Crossing the Line

There is a time at the Chinese place, one with a private menu you must ask for. The guy I work with is much older, banging against sixty. But he is trim and very active. His wife is fat. He leans toward me when the women have gone to the restroom and says, "You're not thinking of getting married, are you? Don't do it, trust me."

All that was long ago.

Now I listen to the agent talking about the big bust.

Everyone wants out. That is what the agent feeds on, this hole he smells in others, the emptiness of old attics with nothing but dust and cobwebs and forgotten trunks.

For a while, the café is a place they meet because they bankroll it as a way to explain their money. The waitress is all smiles even though the customers are few.

I asked her what was the nice part of town where people with money lived.

She said, "Oh, it's all mixed up, all together," and her smile was the size of sunrise.

They are coming, dozens of them, hundreds of them, thousands, millions, billions of them. They are hungry. They are tall and short and brown and white and black and they want what we have or they want what they think we have or they simply want and they are coming, coming over walls, under walls, through the wire, the bathroom window, down from the attic, up from the cellar. This stampede begins before I am born, I see the trampled all around me as a child, poor whites and blacks fleeing the south, displaced persons from the war in Europe, the rural folk of the Midwest driven off the land, grim faces in the mills and slaughterhouses, women with blank eyes hanging clothes on the gray porches facing the elevated trains that stream into the bowels of the city.

And they all want just a little, a taste of the food at the head table. I remember an aunt sewing piecework in a small place by the coking mill. Her dreams were fried chicken, beds of peonies, frilly clothes and very dark nail polish.

Everyone is fleeing the bad days.

There are cabins by the lake, the summer hot velvet in the night. There are hard words, a guy from the Balkans calls another man a kike and then holes up in his cabin at one a.m. With a .45.

The insulted man stands outside throwing rocks at the cabin and screaming threats. He can't marshal a word as hateful as kike. It is not in him.

A crowd forms among the cabins that night, as the rocks fly and the man hides inside with his pistol. The people smoke and hold drinks in their hands. There is a murmuring but no one knows what to say. The man in the cabin with his gun and his hate is beyond their skills. He is something they want to forget even exists.

But they are coming, all broken and maimed and they want what we have and they want what they think we have and what we think hardly matters. Because we refuse to know what they have lived and for that reason we cannot know the hunger inside them or the anger.

There is the time in the kitchen. I wash dishes, I'm fifteen and the air runs a hundred degrees hour after hour. One of the owners also pulls some shifts as a cook and he fucks the waitresses when he can. The other cooks have at them in the cool room over the lettuce crates. Sometimes the waitresses have black eyes from their times between shifts. The guys who work with me in the dishwashing room or as bus boys almost all have records and carry knives.

I get off at one or two a.m. and walk dark city streets with a pack of smokes. I leave the cigarettes on a ledge a block away near the Four Square Gospel Church to save trouble at home. I dream of the waitresses, I savor their scent.

There's an old guy in the back who cleans the lettuce and such.

He hates me.

Finally, he explodes and says, "You don't belong here, you think you are better than us."

I don't know what to say. But I am learning the sound of them coming, all of them coming for what they dream, the women wearing sunglasses over their black eyes, the guys with long-sleeved shirts to cover jailhouse tattoos.

Sometimes we drink in the park and I get free beer.

One night at a party, a bus boy, this one different, this one from a good home, a kid who volunteers on a search and rescue team, he plays tennis and god knows what else. He's in the kitchen and he says something to one of the cooks, a scrawny guy who seems all skin and bone. The little cook knocks him down and pounds his head into the cement floor, and I see the eyes of the guy on the floor and he looks like a bird just snared by a snake and powerless to resist.

They've been coming all my life but there were always stories about more plates at the table, progress and two-car garages.

* * *

The woman stands in six-inch heels spiking her open platform shoes with red nail polish gleaming. She wears beige slacks, a leopard-pattern blouse and makes a few bare notes in block letters as she listens next to her camera man. The man speaking wears a dark blue shirt with black stripes. He says if he is sent back he will be killed. Behind on the wall is a color print of one of his cousins holding his baby—Dionel was twenty-four when they killed him.

The lawyer looks on. He is framed by the son and the mother. The son is very fit, the year in prison has helped. There were times, the lawyer says, when the son thought of suicide.

A reporter asks, "Will you return to Mexico?"

"Right now Mexico is not part of my life."

Six months after Dionel, the father, Servando, goes down.

A month after that, Edgar, a cousin, is slaughtered.

On the wall are happy moments. His father at his sister's high school graduation, she sports a blue cap and gown and clutches her diploma. Her parents flank her, they are all smiles.

Another photograph is of his grandmother, all gray hair and beaming as she leans over to blow out the candles, surrounded by family and with a green balloon emblazoned HAPPY BIRTHDAY!

His grandmother goes nine months after cousin Edgar. It is a family reunion and along with the grandmother, they cut down three aunts, two uncles and a cousin. Eight months after that, another uncle is slaughtered. Then the guy gets a warning and flees across the river and that is how he came to the prison. He entered the country illegally. He had not done his paperwork. He was born on the south side of the river but had spent his life on the north side and never gave it a thought until he got in a scrape, the authorities ran his name and threw him away. After that the killing began. Finally, eleven members of his family were dead.

The mother watches, her face a mask.

The son says that when people are deported from his prison, the Mexican agents turn them over to cartels as soon as they cross the bridge, who in turn call their relatives in the US for ransom money. Sometimes the money is scraped together, sometimes not. Sometimes the kidnapped are not murdered.

No one who leaves the prison takes more than $50 because they can't keep anything when they are given up by the Mexican agents and are kidnapped and tortured.

The press listens and has few questions.

I sit in the back of the room. There is the boy, the mother, the lawyer up front. Then, a bank of cameras. Then the talent, the women who do the standups afterwards before the cameras and they have notebooks or pads and write, always, with very big letters. Then there are the print people with smaller notebooks and they write with smaller letters. Then, the legal staff. And then me. The blood and screams can hardly be heard.

The people listening want to keep a distance from the story being told and I am no different. There is a wall and it is patrolled by the questions we ask and the words we choose.

* * *

There are places I try not to go.

I walk the creek, the hawk screams, I busy myself with observations, make notes about sightings and the first flowers that follow the rain.

There is that night, an October evening, when the family gathers and the killers came in the back door armed with AKs and one of the killers is a woman. The grandmother goes down, some aunts and uncles, a cousin, and it's better to keep a distance from the pain waiting in the front of the room at the press conference, the eleven corpses.

On the creek, the trick is to name the bird, not to be the bird. There are lines and crossing them has a cost. Become the bird and you can never return to being the person you were. Become the grandma full of holes lurching with the old birthday cake and you cannot keep what is happening over there.

A young gray hawk perches on the edge of the field and I see it in the soft light before dawn and the seeping darkness that comes after sunset. I can feel its eyes on me. It is less than a year old but stares with force and leaves a blood trail that soars in the heavens and screams through the most remote sanctuary of the forest, a killer's eyes looking out on a landscape of murder and yet the drive, as in all birds, seems to be always something ahead, the nest, the eggs, the hatchlings, the future.

I hear its scream in the half-light just as dawn seeps over the ridge. I cross a line and join the beasts. A man slides out of the tall grass in the growing dusk, a water jug on his hip, small pack on his back and I cross a line.

On the line, they are always coming, always hungry.

The final question is this: if you cross the line can you bear the breath of life blowing on the back of your neck and then building to gale force until it knocks you flat on the ground? I lie there thinking this must be death and knowing this has to be life or there will be nothing but death.

* * *

The agent talks about when they took down the head of the ring. He says he was surprised by his house. Modular. And in every room, he sneers, a forty-inch screen. In the kitchen, nothing but a sack of potatoes and a sack of beans.

The ringleader drives an '89 Jaguar with bald tires.

"I'm trying to tell you," the agent says with finality, "the guy had no taste."

There is a recent receipt for fifty grand from a casino.

He pays his drivers three grand for moving a load seventy-five miles.

He lacks taste.

Beans, potatoes, big screens, bald tires.

The agent says they were moving two tons a week. A local guy says, "I knew them since they were born, their father was a hard-working man, just a hard-working man and the kids, well, they were around and I always knew when something was up. I'd see girls at the stash house and it was just down the street but they were moving a ton a week, hell, they'd be borrowing money for gas and someone, somebody had vengeance, that's what I think, hell, the one brother got eight and the other twelve and that ain't no plea bargain for moving some grass, no, somebody got vengeance."

And that's all he says.

The clouds hang low, the rains have come and then the creek rises. The ground swells up wet and smears the face as leaves float slowly to earth off the cottonwoods. In the store, the tanned man gets three packs of smokes and a twelve pack, the young cashier leans forward spilling her breasts because it is summer and because she knows what is wanted and all of this, every second of this, vanishes when the agents come and take you away to their cages.

The ravens croak in the pre-dawn gray, the air damp and memories of strawberries well up in my head. I heat some tripe, place the pile on the lip of the creek, watch the black hulks swoop down and remember a day in early May when I enter a farm kitchen with a pail full of strawberries plucked as I crawled on my knees between the rows of dark green leaves and my fingers are smeared red and I reach up to the counter where a porcelain crock rests and take the ladle of cool water drawn from the well and the air still feels the cool of night and the soft damp that will burn off in an hour or so and now the ravens croak and one flies off with a piece of tripe in its bill and I feel nothing less than wonder and want to smear what is left of my life all over the ground and trees and the vault of blue rising about the forest. I walk from the raven and somehow am back in that long-ago kitchen, walk past the crock resting on the old wooden countertop, go into the dining room where fine white curtains with embroidered edges flutter softly in the slight stir of morning, lick my red-stained fingers and look out at the sweep of land—corn, oats, barley, flax, soybeans, wheat, alfalfa, red clover—hear the lowing of the cattle, the cluck of hens. I smell her perfume, feel the soft fabric of her blouse brush my fingers, fall into a well of past aromas and sounds and colors and light, a place that provides safe harbor from what I see just over that ridge, the skies going to fire, the rains burning off before touching ground, trees going yellow then brown, the wind up and at night the moon stares at heaped bones that glow in the cities.

They are coming, there will be plans, speeches, special agents, new guns and walls, still they will come, the mosquitoes and gnats are at my face, first bats of evening, hummingbirds of dawn, a Strauss waltz floats out the door and over the creek, vultures stare from the cottonwoods with red heads and loving eyes and I learn what governments never will know, that there are many ways of being alive. The rose petals falling on the ground, the hardness of her nipple as I brush my fingers against it, the dog worrying a rank scent along the trail, small tracks in the mud, the pad of the lion, they are coming, there are too many of us, still they come, the beasts can barely get to the table, still they come, millions of them, billions of them, hurling through space from some dream in the loins of others.

* * *

The café is folding tables with red tops, green tops, slate-gray tops. The ceiling covered with strips of silver duct tape, the walls slate gray with bas-reliefs of sea horses. The menu leans to tacos—lengua, birria, fish, and cabeza, fish or shrimp soup, fruit drinks. Every face is smiles. Out the window is a twisting street lined with body shops and mechanics. The walls snake up and down the hills about a mile south, twenty to thirty feet high, steel columns filled with concrete, the wall between us and them. No one speaks of this matter.

They are all smiles.

I savor the soup—the family that owns the café makes their own stock. Near the wall, that mile or so to the south, the agents shot down that boy one night. I spoon my soup and I am in Iowa following presidential candidates as they wade into small-town cafés, union halls and county fairs. They hardly matter. The volunteers are packed chockablock in cheap rented offices and working feverishly. I talk to a woman, she is in her twenties, she has come from New York and been here a day. Before she was with another candidate but he failed and now there is this candidate. She does not know a lot about him except that he is in the race and has a shot. Outside a community center, a huge bus idles with the face of a candidate smiling out. Candidates stand scattered about waiting for supporters to flock to their cause.

One day I fled the campaign and the press bus that followed the candidate. I went to a small city and looked at paintings by Grant Wood, drank weak coffee in cafés in empty towns where the family farm had long ago vanished into the sweep of corporate fields. I look for yesterday amid the Holsteins and country taverns, the cisterns of pure water from childhood, the bucket of warm milk carried up from the barn of dawn. At the Amana colonies, I see a cannonball bed and think if I simply crawl onto it, I'll find the faith of our fathers.

I crave the ground of rot that flings mushrooms up overnight, the murderous hoot of the owl on a moonlit night.

Toward twilight, the sun hangs over the oaks and stares through the smoke off the coking plants along the valley. The cattle graze in the low meadow, the screen door lets cooking smells pour into the barnyard. Just off the path is the garden, a wilderness of tomatoes, beans, squash, cucumbers, greens. That is my mother's ground. The two barns, the big garage, those are my father's ground. Women talk in the kitchen, men sit on the porch, flies buzz. The air is August, hints of a coming harvest crackle across cornfields. I feel love. The house lights that now come on one by one, old lamps of brass, a wooden table lamp with the stem spun on a lathe by some dead uncle or cousin, the brass ashtrays fashioned from artillery shells from the war.

Wait, wait, birds are feeding, the leaves rustle, I am losing that long-ago moment when my mother tends the wood stove, my old man sits on the porch with the others, August sags in the heat, and I am a toddler and want to bolt into the growing dark and join the sweep of green raw grass. I sip coffee and read Friedrich Nietzsche: "We ought still to be as close to the flowers, grasses, and butterflies as a child who does not yet reach very far above them. We older people, by contrast, have grown beyond them and have to stoop down to them; I think that the grasses hate us if we confess our love for them."

Yes, I think that is it. I must stoop down to the grass. But still, I do not agree. I do not think the grass hates me. I cannot bear that thought. I can't handle lines, walls, barriers, not anymore. I have gone to the hungers I cannot shake.

The auction is at night under fluorescent lights. They sell coffee and popcorn in the back of the hall. The women eye the items up for bid, the men stand smoking with the blank faces of the poker table. There are no antiques. Everything is old and worn and cheap. My old man bids on a gray headboard with cabinets. He'll keep his loaded .45 and condoms in there. My mother nudges him one night and he bids on two maple end tables for the living room. They left almost everything back in Illinois. The auctioneer barks, hands raise up here and there. Outside the earth cracks under the heat of summer.

Entire lifetimes of tables, chairs, couches, beds, rugs, plates, spoons, cups, orphans all, the men blank-faced, the women anxious—would their man bag the prize?—the faces blue under the fluorescent lights, the auctioneer pumping up the crowd, a world is passing, one with spring mattresses and old brass beds and now there is the future of cheap veneered composite bookcase headboards and lamps are all slender, goose necked and sleek, a world of new castoffs mingling with old stuff from iron days of no jobs and one by one fragments of busted lives go up—this is not an estate sale of treasure antiques—and I am a boy and wonder when I will stand and bid on faded things.

They're coming, more and more, they're coming.

But when they come they are never simply they, they are a face, a smile, eyes unlike any others, there is no they when they come.

The Box

He explains the technique is a box. The people cross the line and then spread out, each one keeping in sight of another, but not moving as a line down a path. Think of a box. They are spread out inside this box and their eyes are fixed on some distant landmark where they will all regroup. On a hill will be the boss. He will call guides who are mingled in with the group. No one knows the exact position of the boss. He never reveals that.

The people cross that line, spread out, move in as individuals but move inside a box.

The agent pauses. He says that is how it is done now by the very best.

They are screaming overhead now. At first I saw one on the bark of a tall cottonwood, the limb angled, the bird black with a yellow hooked bill. I paused in the shadow of an ash. At my foot, the sole of a discarded tennis shoe, those treads all but gone, the canvas top rotted away. To my left were strands of yellow and orange nylon rope. They'd served as the straps on the mochila, the burlap bag backpack used by the Mexicans who had walked the kilos to this point. The debris lines the creek in little pockets off the beaten path. Sometimes I slip into hollows of thickets. There is silence and the castoffs of the tiny camps of the sojourners. Faded soft drink cans, water bottles and fraying lengths of rope.

The hawk pivots its head, then alights and moves down near the dead tree that has become the roost of black vultures. I move in the shadows. Suddenly, a second zone-tailed hawk careens across the blue sky from my right. Then two female mallards flap upstream. I wade in the water, my feet cold.

Zone-tailed hawks often nest near roosts of black vultures. They hide inside the kettles of buzzards. Prey doesn't react to the vultures. When the day warms, the vultures rise up on thermals, the zone-tailed mingle with them. Gnats eat at my eyes.

Overhead, I hear the racket of the young in the heron rookery. The hawks perch on separate limbs and eye me. Since the arrests, hardly anyone comes here. I seldom see a boot print not my own.

I read once that you never see a hawk before it sees you.

A heron lands and feeds.

The old mulberry tree fell and now is a stack of cut wood. The beer garden next to the bar still has some shade. A few hundred yards up the road, seven machines full of agents have a lone Mexican spread-eagle on the hood of his little white pickup.

The nest concerns me. I think it belongs to the zone-tailed hawks but I never see them on it; their call is long and piercing.

The man in the beer garden says there is a zone-tail nest on that stretch of creek. Of the ropes and rotting burlap, he says that is all from the time before the big bust when the agents scooped up about two dozen and said they'd taken down a major ring.

“They’d have parties out there,” he says, “pizza and beer as they waited.”

Near one of the cache sites I count forty-two black Mexican vultures. Some are drinking from the stream but most are sitting on the branches of dead trees sunning.

They triangulate and finally get the big guy who for more than ten years has smuggled people without mishap. He is the obsession of the agent. And then he goes down softly like a whisper. He has crossed the line this time and is directing his illegals by radio. The authorities triangulate his signal, and take him. It is that simple.

He talks freely to the agent when debriefed.

He got a bad meth habit, he says, and so about three or four months ago he vanished into treatment. Clean, he returned to his work.

For years, the smuggler had loomed large in the agent’s mind as a figure of power and mastery.

Now he learns that after fourteen years of smuggling, the man had climbed the rungs of his criminal ladder and was still earning less than the agent.

One day I am trying to find the nest of a gray hawk. I see the pair often and hear them screaming. But I cannot get a fix on their nest. I know it is near, I have seen them rise up and chase off other hawks. The heat has not come on yet and the soft light of morning lingers under the trees. I see her first. She is walking two fat Labradors on leashes and has a pistol on her hip. Then he appears on his ATV with a rifle and shotgun racked behind his head, a pistol also on his hip.

Then he tells me of the danger.

Two women were down by the creek, he says, and a deer came to drink and then suddenly a lion leapt from the bushes and dragged the deer off, just like that.

He says, "That's why I wear a pistol when I drive the road on my ATV."

And I know he means the dirt road that meanders for about three miles as a back way to town and the saloon.

And he says there is the danger of the wets moving through, the illegals streaming up from the south. He produces a small rusty tin, the kind poor Mexicans pack so that when hunger finally cannot be denied they keep going by eating a little fish.

I nod.

Fear, not just a word, but a wave with scent and barbs that tear the flesh, fear rising up and then the dogs are on you, the grip loosens, panic comes, your face vanishes beneath the wave and there is the crack of the rifle, the break in the levee and the river racing into freedom, the long skid before the car sails off dead man's curve, a thing that can be in the flesh or in the air or on the ground or on the waters and this sensation makes the people into the mob, the picnic into the lynching party, the future into a ruin, and fear can be had in the midst of plenty on a Saturday under the bright lights, or fear can come with empty hours of darkness and the faint footfall of the beast, the brown wall of water as the creek comes up in the moonless night and then. I get up and go out there barefoot and naked, the ground soft underfoot, the roar of the water and yet a stillness as everything living, every living thing pulls back in the wave of fear and the ash, sycamore and cottonwood of the bottomland fight to stay aloft in the thunder of the flood and I sit on the ground and feel the high water and the fear of the flood—the deer move up on the hillside, I have seen this when the big water comes by day—and the air flows raw and fresh, air that has just been blasted by the storm and the world also has been born again and no one is safe and meteors fall, love slaps a body blind, but there is more, maybe it is not fear at all, it is a hesitation, a string of questions that paralyze and then this frozen moment becomes life for people and it all goes on unnoticed and without concern. I want free of such feelings, I want the feel of leaves on the forest floor, the musk coming from wet earth, the swing of the hips as the girls go by in their summer clothes, slow wing flap of a heron bringing food back to the nest, the edge of the storm raking down the valley trembling the cottonwoods.

Crossing the Line

He comes over the wall and lands in my life.

He's got the body of a convict who spent his time in the yard with the iron pile. He's forty, blond hair, blue eyes and winning smile. Sometimes the trouble comes from the bottle, but more often from the pipe.

He keeps writing poems about a place called Knife Street where life is a blade and anger. He's shown his poems down at the university and they've encouraged him but he doesn't believe them because he doesn't trust them because he doesn't see any scars on their bodies or hear the scars in their talk. His mom was Indian or part Indian, his dad a drunk and then gone. He married the rich girl, had the big house, stables, money. Once I helped him find the satellite image of the place and all he talked about were the trees—loblolly, ash and how he planted 'em all and how they'd grown so. Eventually, his hungers got the best of him and he hit her and did drugs and it all went to hell and he went to prison.

Things can be fine and then they are gone, just like that—house, woman, stables, the trees you planted.

I stand watching the creek rise. There is a crack and a forty-foot cottonwood tumbles to earth and this morning in the gray light that cottonwood figured on living forever. Two days later the water rose again, the toppled tree shuddered and began to move downstream. The water got higher and higher, the day-old fence put in after the last torrent vanished in the first fifteen minutes. And still the water keeps coming from canyons and hills. There is no safe bet by a creek. The water stays brown for days. The herons and kingfishers move until it clears. The watercress is scoured away.

He sits there sipping a beer and enjoyed a rolled smoke and looks up brightly, "They say I'm bipolar."

Then, he snorts and drains his beer.

He is very bright, borrows books from me, scorns television and sees the world through cracks in his head. He is climbing down a ladder. The busted marriage was not enough. Prison was not enough. When I first met him he had a flatbed truck with a bad starter, a chainsaw and a ladder. He also had tailor-made cigarettes then.

He took me once to see the truck—his landlord had impounded it and kept it in the yard for back rent. Before that he'd lost it for awhile for dead plates—they'd pulled him over and ran his name, found the outstandings, tossed him in and during the thirty days the truck was towed to a yard and he had to move heaven and earth to get it back. Christ, that story went on and on because it was such a damn good truck, he insisted and besides he couldn't get work unless he could haul the dead wood away and so that truck, that was life, well, maybe not exactly but without the truck there was no work, and without work the pipe stayed empty and without the pipe the woman vanished.

But then she did anyway now and then.

He'd bring her over at times. She worked as a practical nurse and had some heft and very quick eyes, the kind of eyes you knew would ask to use the bathroom and the kind of eyes you knew would open the medicine cabinet and would vacuum everything with the hint of an upper or downer.

Sometimes he'd get angry about her, how she took his drugs and stuff, and sometimes he'd get angry how she'd go off when he had no drugs and then he stopped, and would not say much about what she did when she went off and he had no drugs. Sometimes he'd bring her and her brother, a little ferret-faced guy who was very polite and seemed to scan every object to determine what was most portable.

They were all rungs on the ladder, things essential if he were to reach his destiny and he was sure of his destiny even if it had yet to be revealed to him.

He looms as he speaks, his huge arms and chest the armor over his busted life. He tries to be reasonable, he is in a chair, the walls are bookcases, he's got a free beer, he's smoking, for a brief while he's a regular guy, just leaning back and shooting the breeze but he can never hold that moment, never keep a grip on this calm, something always boils out of him, and anger at cops and people who look down on him and people with money who don't work as hard as he does and at the government that doesn't give a damn about him—he checks about rehab and finds he must wait months for a slot and for a man with a pipe that means never, never, never, and then he falls into a litany of broken dreams and bad cops.

He learns about trees in prison, this woman taught a class and that is how he got into tree trimming and he is an encyclopedia of tree diseases. He can't look at a tree on the place without telling me it is ailing and the only cure is for him to do some cutting on it. As time goes on and the truck goes and the ladders, also the bicycle and then there is only the chainsaw, he still keeps working, swinging from limb to limb in the tree like a great ape.

Then he is gone for a month or more.

He comes back and says he walked ten miles a day. The cell was eight feet long, he'd do about 659 laps to a mile, 6600 a day just to be sure of his ten miles and he did it every day, every single day, because that's how you do time and keep control and he's going to be clean now, he's going to go back to the Carolinas and I give him a few bucks and he's gone. He takes a bus to Amarillo. He gets off, looks out at the plains and wonders why he is there and so comes back. He finds a dog, the perfect friend. The woman is gone, the truck and all that gone, the pipe, the pipe seems to remain. He and the dog have a life. He walks out to the edge of town, waits with the dog for a ride. The cops bag him. The dog goes to the pound and by the time he finally gets out of jail, well, the dog has been destroyed, best damn dog he ever knew.

Each day the defeated seem to grow in number. Nobody is counting, but still they are growing in number and each day they get more angry and they know they are defeated but they don't see themselves as a group, just a wound. They hide their wounds because being taken down is shameful, and they lie about their pain and they say things that make it sound like their lives are on the upswing and that they are part of the bigger thing that surrounds them, the people with jobs and good liquor and legal habits. They say that they're getting by and hey, let's have a beer, and everyone belongs to some vague middle and no one will admit that the undertow is taking them, the car will be repossessed, the rent is two months late, and all they want to do is drink and blot out what they see roaring toward them and he sits there and talks about poetry or projects or the diseases trees are prone to and he's going to get clean, get a truck and fire up the business of his life, thank you very much.

* * *

She's barely twenty. The mom is not right, something about her head, so she stays home and takes pills. The dad cuts meat in a market. The girl, she has a job with a big chain, she works the delicatessen, it pays $8.08 an hour and that doesn't pay for much, so she lives at home.

This she tells the cops as they make her stay in a room and give them what they want.

Do drugs?

Oh, no sir. I don't drink either, sir.

How did you get involved?

Well, I ran into this girl I knew at a party and she told me about it.

What was her name?

She just told me, that's all.

These calls on your phone? Is that her?

No, no, sir, that is someone else, someone who has nothing to do with it.

It goes on like that, page after page, the clock ticking, the questions repeating and repeating because the people with the good jobs and the pensions and paid vacations need meat to feed their habit and their habit is putting people in cages. The girl goes on about how she did the first run in December because Christmas was coming and she had no money for her family and they paid her $3000 for driving the load seventy-five miles and looking innocent at the one checkpoint and then she did another and another and she quit because she had a new job that started in a week or two and this would pay her ten dollars an hour.

And they called and she said yes she would do it one more time and that time she got caught. Before she got to the checkpoint her boss calls on the phone and says, hey, don't break the speed limit the cops are waiting and so she is careful but still this cop pulls her over and says you were speeding and she knows she was not but still they take her to the room and the questions begin and they keep asking the same thing, like who is this person who keeps calling on the phone and she tries to tell them nothing, she really tries but they just keep asking.

She tries, she really tries.

But they are hard to beat. They have the law.

Later, I'm talking with the agent, the man who is appalled that the leader drove an old car with bald tires and appalled that in his house they found nothing but a sack of beans and a sack of potatoes.

I ask about the girl.

He says it can be terrible, that sometimes they put a gun to their head to make them drive.

There have to be lines, sharp, defined things, thirty-foot walls, rolls of concertina wire, the saved and the damned, the country club and the others, the humans and the beasts, hard lines, race, class, and let us see that passport, stand over there, open your bag, do not get out of the vehicle, license please, you wait, lines, cages, laws, borders, rules, always rules and all of the rules are the same: we got the power and you don't. But the important thing is not the power, no, the important thing is the line that says us and them, that says you are the wrong color or you are the wrong species or you are not us and so the agents come and the walls and the guns and the laws and the mausoleums full of lawyers and judges, endless ways to put you down and if you complain put you out forever, and this can be done because you run drugs, leave old nylon rope and spent burlap bags along the creek, because you have no money and you are not going to have money because we won't pay you much and so you are the criminal and cross the line and go down or you are the illegals coming north or climbing out of a container in a port and here is what is wrong with you, you didn't pick the right parents and this will not be forgiven, and this is true of the Mexican or the Chinaman or the zone-tailed hawk or the lion padding softly down the creek in the night, eyes huge with hunger for the fresh blood of the deer. Nobody is forgiven who crosses the line and helps other bloods and says the other breeds of man and beast are their equals and their brothers and their sisters.

This is never forgiven.

So it is written in the books of law.

That is the moment, when you know you can never be forgiven, when you know they have made your heart illegal, that is the moment you cross the final line into freedom land and become one with trees dirt fangs musk high water and howls in the night and cease to have solutions and cease to think of issues and cease to listen to anything but the rustle of leaves, the songs in gray light of morning, the sap slowly gurgling to the canopy and the messages of mice and snakes on the dust of the earth, then you know what to do and who you are and realize there is no going back.

The time for meetings is over. There will be no big fix. There will only be yes or no. There will be the lesson of the hawk or the reprimands of the cops.

They are coming, walls or no walls. You must be on a side or be nothing at all and if you do not side with beasts and other bloods you belong to the world of triumph, a world that leads to death.

Eleven slaughtered, all from one family, and in this courtroom in the detention center the government argues that does not mean the defendant is in any danger if he's tossed back into the place that ate his father and uncles and aunts and cousins and grandmother, no, there is no evidence of any danger there, not a bit and as for the girl who made $8.08 an hour with the weekly total held down to thirty hours to keep the benefits in line and who ran a load seventy-five miles for $3000 come Christmas time, well, she had a choice. For example, she could have gone to law school and become like the prosecutor piling charges on her head, or like the judge, she had a choice and she made her choice. Bailiff send in the next one.

Crossing the Line

A yellow female tanager climbs the dead branch of the ash in the throat of the canyon. A gray hawk lifts and moves across the gap to an oak in the soft light of the coming storm. The red male summer tanager flits past.

There is a sound when the waters come up, a roar mixed with the crashing of rocks and logs, and this sound is not frightening despite our claims later but beckoning and in the night I always rise and go toward it and stare with wonder and in the summers I go naked to the brown wall storming across my life. In the dawn you will see the damage—trees uprooted, fencing gone, dead animals floated down from above, and the vultures wheel overhead as they survey their new bounty. The air crackles, fresh from the lungs of the storm. Fallen leaves carpet the soggy ground and there are no prints on the bottomland, none at all, sometimes nothing for a day or two because the quick moved to high ground when they hear the roar and the rolling and tumbling and the slow are dead and will make no more tracks. The birds' song rises with the sun and the creek eats new wood and plant and soil and rock and spends days weeks months years digesting the meal and fingering out a new channel and then thirty years later you are back and the tanager streaks and the gray hawk lifts up and there is no trace of that monster flood that scoured the bottomland, and life carpets the old wounds with grace and lust.

I hear a chuff chuff chuff, look up and see the blue and white chopper full of agents stalking the line. I stumble on two black plastic water bottles abandoned by illegals.

Miles run all over my face. I have traveled back to where I began on a farm by a creek with fish jumping and just down the hills the big stacks at the mills filling the blue sky with smoke. Now I am that man without a country or a flag—I have gone to ground, right where I started as a child sprawled in the dirt and for me now it is always spring and beginning and all the miles behind me, all those dead ends and closing time drinks and women, that is some other season before I left and joined what I find in the canyon, the tumbling of the flood, the boom of sound off rock walls and the trill of birds that live and die so fast and matter more than presidents, more than all of the presidents.

You cross the line, you become a traitor.

The zone-tailed adult comes in softly, lands on the limb and the fledgling rises up with excitement.

Young herons line the creek and call out in hunger for their parents. They are about the same size as the adults but there is something within them that needs nurturing and there is something within the parents that keeps them flying miles to the lake and then miles back with fish for their giant offspring.

A yellow-billed cuckoo moves through the coyote willows, they've come north to feed on hairy caterpillars that show up in the thickets when the rains finally begin. They live furtive and fast lives, the young barely born it seems before they explode in feathers and flight, yes, yes, yes, the world is clean and open and ride, ride, ride.

PART II
Music and Silence

All you have to do is touch the right key at the right time and the instrument will play itself.

J. S. BACH

The aim and final reason of all music should be none else but the glory of God and refreshing the soul. Where this is not observed there will be no music, but only a devilish hubbub.

J. S. BACH

The fingers caress the keys, then a wind roars off the granite face of the cliff. I curl on the rock, on the desert plain below lie the bones of earlier wars—the dead from the conquest, the dead from '49, the dead from the big wars, the dead from little border wars, the dead from drug wars, the dead from the wars against the poor.

Charles Ives rips through Piano Sonata No. 1, something he never quite feels right about and finally gives up on after the Great War. The wind, I think, is coming through the spaces between the notes of that sonata. The dead below start to stir as the notes bang against each other and Ives hears a brass band in his head, he's always hearing a brass band swinging down the street or some hymns flowing out the church door come a Sunday. The sonata matches the bones rattling below as the skeletons dance in the wind to "Bringing in the Sheaves," and my father set the record in his county for stacking shocks of sheaves when the harvest came and he did this though he was a landless man in a county of hamlets and farmers and Charles Ives hammers his piano and the old hymn goes "Bringing in the sheaves, bringing in the sheaves, We shall come rejoicing, bringing in the sheaves," and my father would rather go to hell than enter a church but he worked those fields and gathered in the sheaves even though his family huddled in a small house in town stuffed with ten children and a ne'er-do-well father and patient mother and I see three turkeys by the creek in early morning light, two deer pause in the tall grass and stare, the yellow-breasted chats will not shut up, I hear one before dawn in the barely gray light still washed with moon, and there is the matter of exposition, development and recapitulation that I am supposed to attend to but four blue herons fly over together and this clustering I have never seen before, at dusk three mallards skim the trees heading toward the lake, the air is full of smoke from fires in Mexico and I hear old man Ives pounding out "Bringing in the Sheaves," his first sonata sings inside my head and the skeletons will not stop their dancing.

I am told a note on a piano begins to decay as soon as it is struck. I sense a person begins to decay at birth, that some clock starts counting down and this timepiece is buried in the body and cannot be reset. I know that the future and the past are all beyond my reach. I know all the moments are here now with me as Ives plays and the wind blows.

Do Nothing

Blood drips from the stone as I sip black coffee. Men and women claw this rock face desperate for stagnant water trapped in stone holes. Their hands bleed, they fall, their bodies thud on desert soil, bones, bones, bones at the bottom of the cliff. I lean forward and they are gasping, casualties of the Gold Rush of '49.

Falling rock clatters as bighorns move above me. God is far away. Yesterday, when I could still move, I met a young ram on the trail, the broken foreleg dangling. I moved aside as it staggered past me. We both kept our silence. I wanted to help but could not imagine what help might mean. It was fifty miles to a road.

Just below are the graves of nameless people who fell from the rock in trying to reach water. The little mounds wear down in the wind. Soon the bones will rise up and dance away.

A military jet roars just above the level of the desert scrub. A few miles south, the open wound of the border seeps. I lie there for days, my leg throbbing. I see hawks riding the sky below me. I am a long walk from stores, streets and houses. In my delirium I see things happening—a drug deal gone bad, a group down in the heat and dying, the arrest of illegal Mexicans by legal Americans. I do not move. I seem paralyzed.

Life is not about knowing right from wrong. It is about doing the right thing.

The dry bite of desert air, sky blue, sun bright.

That is the core: I do nothing.

There is a lawyer, a man with no feet—let me think a moment—yes, there is also a priest and a nun. And the man who slides down the slope and comes out of the tall grass. There are probably more, I am sure there are more. Yes, yes, there is the woman facing that surgery, there is my old man in the back room dying. And more. I am forgetting them at the moment. My head gets crowded and so I get rid of people. But they come back. I think I have erased them and then they come back. Sometimes, after midnight when the owls hoot under moonless skies. The lawyer, he's got the cancer and he's got clients seeking shelter from the storm. The cancer, that eats but does not earn and the people fleeing death and government and black weather, they don't pay. He's getting bony now, and a little frail at times. He'd been a bull of a man hard to keep on a leash or home at night. I can see him in the bar pouring down those martinis with joy on his face, the way a man should drink if he is in this world.

A Swainson's hawk slices low over my head on its way north from the wintering grounds in Argentina, the red collar framing the white face and I feel the turbulence of thousands of such hawks as they stream through Mexico and Central America, smell the salt air off the sea at Veracruz, and black coffee in Xalapa, the swish of the cloth as the women swing by and flowers brushing my skin, and there is the time I go to the suicide bars, bad places with desperate angers and I look for trouble because I want to hit someone.

But a man comes out of the tall grass. But a man has no feet. But a man dabs at his gum because of the cancer.

That's the story here: I do nothing. And I meet people who act. And then I have to face what I am.

I hear voices, some soft, some harsh.

I smell perfume.

I drift off, people tell me I vanish before their eyes. A ghost in my own life.

Silence

I get a report on the man in the burning cabin. His head is separate from his body, the message says, because he blew his brains out. The message ends simply: "He's toast."

The ram walks down the trail toward me, the right foreleg broken, blood dribbling on the ground, the eye a fire of desire. I get down below the trail as the sheep staggers past. The broke bill dove feeds, feathers ruffled because it can no longer preen. I am certain they will live.

I am a question mark.

She is very soft. She leans forward and says, hey, is that any way to greet a friend?

This is wrong. This is written in the holy books.

The song sparrow haunts the creek, melody rippling across my face, all this before the man slides out of the tall grass and asks his question, all this before I face facts. The male song sparrows fling down challenges with their riffs and if they are going to get physical and attack, then their song gets soft, very soft and this throws their anger into the blue sky.

I am calm now and can finally hear the silence coming down in this country of the dead. There is the faint buzz in the air as drones drift overhead on one side of the line. On the other side, there are muffled cries from the murdered and with each hour these cries become more difficult for me to hear. All over the nation to the south, messages are vanishing from radio and television and newspapers and an economy of crime grows, an economy of torture, murder, extortion and kidnapping. Silence smothers voices.

There is more silence. The birds fall dead from the sky, silence, the rivers die, silence, the men stand in the morning light in the back of a picket-lined flatbed truck, the faces masked against the winter chill and they are shoulder to shoulder like tenpins as they head for vegetable fields groaning with produce for tables across the line to the north, dust rising, their faces hidden by bandanas, the sun barely up, the endless rows waiting for them. Silence.

The cold flow licks the gravel at the bottom of the stream, the red, gray and brown rock soft under the clear water. They came this way, microbes, spores, seeds, conquerors, some now embedded in the stream, particles in the faint murmur of the meandering tongue. The ash and walnuts cluster, the cottonwoods own the banks and here and there, sycamores cling to big rocks. An orange-crowned warbler darts in and out of the brush, faint streaks racing down the tiny chest *and this woman in the long ago, she survives the death camps fashioned for Jews in Europe and she returns to the country home her family had in Czechoslovakia, knocks on the door, a fat man answers, the new owner and he shouts, "So you've come back! Oh no! That's all we needed!" and the woman walks away, goes down into the woods, lies on the green moss of the ground and lets bird song pour into her life* and summer tanagers move through the trees, thick-trunked hackberries loom like some dreaded forest in childhood dreams, raw scents float up from the barn, everything is very strange and yet very simple, the chickens peck in the yard, cattle low, dark waters of the creek moving from the light into the bend under the trees, dragonflies, dragonflies, and the crows caw with an urgent tone, doves race into the shelter of the trees and suddenly the hawk swings through, a dark shadow on a blue sky day and just south, hardly a stroll, the drones hunt all but silently, coming over the hills without warning, their empty eyes sending messages to hunters in air-conditioned rooms, doves hiding in the trees, a man slides down the slope, comes out of the tall grass *and by October the lake finally warms, Michigan so big and deep it takes a hundred and ten years to empty and fill its hunger and with Indian summer the water feels good against the skin and first the gravel near shore, then a band of sand then more gravel, a pattern of time and motion under foot, and the big waters rise, I body surf and vanish into the tumble of waves and feel the hands of drowned sailors on sunken ore boats out there under the gray waters of November as the last hopes come rolling onto the beach before the ice walls of winter take the shore and time bends and becomes physical, the sand and rocks scoring my skin* and a Northern harrier bursts through the coyote willow along the stream, a group of green-winged teals lifts up in alarm, then realizes they are not prey and drops down and all the while the great blue heron continues its hunt, one leg lifts as it stares into the sheen of water for fish, killdeer on the mudflat, crows wandering the sands, and I think I can reach what I had and left behind, that certainty that each day can make good, that birdsong means more than the talk in the saloons and the scent of a woman is better than the fields of spring and I am brought up short by the sounds of cranes overhead, they are leaving for the north, the lust rises and they go their thousands of miles to the ground of dancing, love, nesting and then the young, all this past my sight and those first unsteady steps out the door and into the barnyard and past the henhouse, the garden, the pig sty, the dairy barns, on and on, tumbling down the green slope to the creek, the carp jumping, green scum sleeping in the quiet folds of water, cattails bold, crows robbing the orchards, the men pounding in fence posts to claim the land from the land, and then the limestone cliffs and the dive to the laze of the bottomland *and at the eight-sided crossing a Russian officer is gunned down in Budapest along with a Russian soldier, a Hungarian girl dies with them, the killer's charred body found in an attic and it is 1946, the reactionaries threaten the revolution, yes, yes, the newspapers scream this out and no one ever knows all the reasons but they do learn one reason, the boy who became the charred body loved the girl who was with the Russian officer and so he fired and killed the Russians and the girl and then killed himself, all this before the organs of government made him into something useful, an enemy of the people that justified an iron fist in the face of other people* and a front roars in, the birds are crazed with hunger, the cold falls down, wind is up, leaves flee the trees, a grackle sings against the growing storm, and she smiles, hands me the wine in a thin-stemmed glass, the globe all red and hungry, the fire crackles, meat roasts on a spit, the world is music, herons drift past the window and then comes night, stars talking in whispers, the moon a blare of words, and the river runs past the huge monument to Christopher Columbus, her severed head is displayed there at dawn along with her keyboard, she was writing things she thought others should know and now she will no longer do this, and the river runs past Nuevo Laredo, once I stood there on the bank with terrified migrants from Central America, people coming north and stalled by guards across the river and the killers within Nuevo Laredo, the man slides down the slope, comes out of the tall grass and says . . . the wine glass feels good in my hand, the fire crackling, she leans forward, and this is an early moment in the new silence, and the men from Central America beg for food, I hand out money and stare at the river between where they beg and where they live in their dreams, and I feel the hot breath of desire and can do nothing but face it down by the river *and the dinner party is long, the house large and up in the hills where people with money stare down at the valley of people with less money and two of the women say that if you enter the Amazon some of the tribes can steal your mind and you come back a zombie and others at the table make knowing nods, and I leave, she follows and hands me two bags and later, hundreds of miles south when I am on the drug coast of Sinaloa I open them as the drug dealer stands by the window, gun shots ringing out over the city, and speaks of his fears and how one deal more or two and he will be out, he cannot take it anymore, his stomach is all but gone, he says, and the shots ring out over the city, they do every night and I open the bags, one has her panties, leopard pattern, and the other shaved hair, and the drug dealer never notices, the shots ring out, I have come some kind of full circle and I know it*, the man slides down the slope, hungry and beaten, he comes out of the tall grass, I cannot seem to erase that moment and I have been trying since the first second I saw him, just as I had tried to erase similar moments for years, a northern harrier bursts through the willows and almost touches my head, flocks of meadowlarks move through the dry grass, the wind comes up, the air goes brown, I choke and cannot see more than a mile, if that, roadrunners hide in thickets and do not see my approach, a redtail hawk careens in and suddenly crows lift up to mob it, the ducks huddle—American wigeons, mallards, northern shovelers, green-winged teals—killdeer dance, and I cannot erase the man who slides down the slope and comes out of the tall grass because I hear voices in my head, the voice of a man recounting his drive deep into Mexico, how he traveled very public roads during bright hours, how he hit the back byways in the hours just before dawn when the roadblocks were unlikely to be up, how the people he meets whisper their lives now, how the silence is becoming the country as the reporters fall mute or vanish, how the dead go uncounted, you can't go home again, not to that home but you can come here, and here is full of screams and of silence, my God, the wind is up, I become a wall of dust and fly and then tumble into the chasm where my dreams can live, the walls glow with musical notes, a rattlesnake picks the guitar with its fangs, the supple body making chord changes on the fretwork, voices, they are all around me, the voices floating over the strange guitar music, she says she is calling from a stairwell in a tower in some city in Texas and her stockings are beige, she says this, and she is thinking of me and she is wearing no panties, she says this, she has light-colored nipples and once she sat up with her blouse off and said "my breasts should be enough for anyone, just look at my breasts" and her skin is clear and soft and every Sunday without fail she is in church, her voice raised in song, a soft voice full of soft vowels, a voice like syrup and she says "don't hurry, just look at my breasts," this silence descends to the south of me, voices fall still, people vanish, a terror seeps out of the sand and rock and covers the dreams and mountains and deserts, her voice soft, the scent clear, her breasts close and warm and I struggle to raise up, there are miles to go before that sleep, and a woman is on the floor reaching up and if I lean down then am I failing myself and becoming simply a creature of the senses? And if I become a creature of the senses is that the wrong path? And what is the right path? South, over there, the vast silence spreads and Brandon Estaban vanishes on the 29th, so does Gualberto and Geraldo and Estaban, and then there are lists of names on the wind, my God this dust is choking me and she says she is on the stairwell in a tower and she is not wearing panties, yes, none at all she says in the sweet voice, and Nitza Paola vanishes and so does Jose Angel and Juan Pablo and Irene Rocio and it seems the army has taken them but can no longer find them or so it is said, and her hand reaches up from the floor, and this voice says just look at my breasts and I am outside in the rain, I have tired of the bar, and she leans over and yes yes yes and the voices somehow scream even though a vast silence smothers the land, still, the army is taking them and the screams pierce my life and what should I do?

I feel her warmth, ah, that scent, I want to return to that place—*the man is killed outside the courthouse, I met him at the wake, they say it is a contract hit*—she is on the stairwell or she is walking by my side and smiles float from her lips and dance across the blue sky, *a kestrel dives, pins a house finch to the ground, the bird looks up at the hooked bill that will tear it apart and the morning light falls from heaven and then the kestrel lifts with the still-living house finch in its talons and I watch* and this is forbidden, and I put down my drink and ask am I committing suicide by living inside a society that kills the ground under my feet when I should be taking up arms against the society that kills the ground under my feet and there is a bond in a healthy society that holds us together and keeps us from killing ourselves or others, a common shared feeling for each other and the ground around us and this died, died for me, died in the eyes of others and the laws and rules cease to play with my life, and my life has been decades of the wars of fear against people who had ideas on the not-approved list, the wind comes up again, vultures rock in the gale and I weaken and weaken and care for nothing but myself and even at that wish that I ceased to exist and the wind becomes my life, the feel of it stroking my hair, scouring my skin with sand, the roar of sound flooding my brain, pebbles under the clear tongue of the stream, dust grinding my face off, and there is this story I am told of a reporter sitting in a café and writing notes because, she says, they are listening now to everything and when I hear this I am stunned because I can find no one that listens to anything, not even the songs that fall like shiny coins from the throats of birds at dawn, I live in a suffocating silence where words sometimes die in the throat because of a fear of the police or the agents or simply of a them never defined, but mainly the words die from a lack of caring and vanish into the mists, a Cooper's hawk careens near my head and moves under the tree, this is a kind of stuttering I come to realize, a way to sooth myself, and yes, I see the Cooper's hawk and I seize on this moment to reassure myself that life is worth living because the bird on the wing believes. A woman's warm hand touches me. My old man dying in the back room.

I believe every sunrise and I remember the smell of wet grass, the color of robins, and rustle of leaves on the big oaks that outlive nations, all this comes with each sunrise.

I move like a child, all rubber bones and bounce and delight, all this in the sunrise.

But now I am dead weight.

The End Time is now behind us. We begin afresh. The things we feared we now become. The things we abandoned now stalk our new lives. The air is warm, the beasts mainly bone, the news is old and tells us to repent and to enjoy and to submit. The authorities hide in the castle keep. We must sharpen our pikes and pay them a visit. The rivers die of thirst, the deserts burn, flames lick the night sky, mountains tumble down, trees go brown, then fall, the lakes, they all burn, the ocean comes near and the land slides under its wet tongue.

Love

Her slender hand reaches up from the cold floor and tugs on my trousers. Her eyes pools of fear, hunger, and lust. My old man is dying on the bed. His eyes grind with pain. He refuses any medication, his breath a rasp sawing through the dim light of the back room. He does not complain. He does not say much of anything since they mutilated his mouth.

There is no way out of here.

Gray clouds scud past but refuse to give rain. The world was entering the seventh day of the creation when that first mist comes off the seas, then clouds form, rain falls and God sits back finally satisfied with His work. A prairie falcon wheels overhead, the herons wait for fish. Under the moon coyotes yip at the stars.

Her scent lingers, my father's deathbed sounds hang in the air, the grass of my first spring floods my senses. I lurch through the trees. Two wild turkeys stand by the creek, a raven croaks over my head, she drops her pants and lies down on the soft grass of summer.

The buses roar by in the rain splashing me as their headlights hunt through the dark of city streets. My shoes feel wet. I walk for hours.

I smell her perfume.

Feel the cold metal of a gun.

Tables of ballistics are the sacred charts of wisdom in my youth. Long guns beckon dreams of elk bugling at dawn, deer moving softly through the fall woods of rut, the flash of antelope on the yellow grass of the mesas. I stare at racks of armaments in stores and think life will be all smooth paths and blue sky if I acquire a .220 Swift, a .243, a .264 Magnum, and a .270 for elegant hunts in the Rockies for sheep on the crags. I savor the smell of gun oil. The world I am born into feels dead and contained, the air stale, windows closed. In my mind guns explode all this and lead into the wild.

Look down at the snake flattened on the dirt road.

Cool brass in pocket, the ground crumbled rock, slopes steep with thorns, shadows and eyes seeing through me into my secret heart. I stumble forward for the thing past the bonds of family and work and school and laws, hope that the crack of a rifle will tear a hole in the universe and I will slip through that fresh wound and spin dazed in space as I wheel to a new heaven and a new Earth.

The piano plays in my head, the keys slammed, the notes ringing in my brain. Pounding music the noise of my life. Now it grows. I no longer try to silence it or keep it secret. Tides lap the shore, sunrises bleed into the day. The piano never stops. There are bad moments, people yelling.

The piano rolls, barrelhouse style.

He says when he kills he feels a kind of regret for taking a life but afterwards he feels nothing and that is not right.

Fingers flying along the keys.

She sits in the lounge and opens her legs to the room with a smile in the hard afternoon light of the desert.

Soft touch of the late sonatas.

She leaves, the click and soft thud of the motel room door, and never a word about it, not even with our eyes.

I have spent my life seeking to cross over to some other side but I never understood what that would mean until it happened, and so for a long time gone I was sidetracked by the feel of the flesh, the flash of her smile and the thunder of the guns that brought me to the dark woods.

Voices speak.

The voice says, "I hope I won't be one of those women who need a lot of men."

The voice says, "You may think she loves you but you didn't see her here with that guy."

The voice says, "I don't think we should be doing that now."

The voice says, "I want you now."

The sounds of death make me hungry for life. I reach out and crave to be touched because like everyone else on earth I have fought my way through fog banks of cold lonely since birth.

I am in the crazy place and she looks up from the sink with gleaming eyes, the flash of smile and her speech is fast, she's been here off and on for seven years since—and now her fingers fly and she digs into her hair, flaps her open sweater back and forth, does head bobs with the sentences—deportation because her parents kept sending her to the state facility but eventually she attacked that officer and then they sent her back because she was born in Juárez, came north at age five, not legal, not legal at all, and with the pills she is okay for awhile but her parents would take her to the state hospital when she was violent and in Juárez she moved in with her grandmother but then she beat the old lady bad and was out on the street and well she worked behind that bar downtown but there is nothing there but whorehouses and the last time she came back here to the asylum in the desert full of locos after they had raped her bad and she was limping from the beating and now she is getting off the drugs because they are bad for your organs, you know?

I listen to her as the clatter of the kitchen work goes on—

a hundred and twenty crazy people must be fed here three times a day—and I feel her manically reaching out—"I'm bipolar," she smiles—to paint her life across my face. She is twenty-eight and just a few weeks ago, she met the guy, yes, the guy, and he's in the asylum and she is in love and kind of recovered from her last visit to the world and the gang rape and beating.

I stumble forward seeking love or something I cannot name, something warm that fills a hole in me, something like the nuzzling by a puppy or the first fresh scent in the spring, something never found in a bottle or a conversation or a sermon, something I missed on the first day when I drew breath and yet knew I could find and have never doubted is just ahead of me if I can only keep going.

Her words come out in a torrent, the drugs, the bad times when she is violent, the smile flashing against the smell of the asylum where cleaning people up is a task without end and I can barely listen because I want someone to reach out to me and yet I fail when someone does, when she begins broadcasting her life because of the wound that is her life and her smile flashes, the words come faster and faster and go under the waves of her wonder.

In the yard it is late morning when the photograph is taken—there are four men, the addict from Los Angeles, me, the addict now minister from the gutters from Juárez, the cop from the states seeking faith in a godless world and the old one who is beckoned over, an ancient madwoman not five feet tall wrapped in old black clothes, the face peering out from the tunnel of a shawl with wary eyes and then the shutter clicks and there we are and I stare at the image and realize the crazy woman is more at peace with the world than the rest of us and feel the cold chill in my gut as I know suddenly I am alone and that no one in the crazy place is alone, no one there is without a warm embrace on their life and that the ice house of modern life has moved into my life and I must follow the crazy people and the lost and the damned and the scorned if I am to find my way home.

All the while I hear voices and songs and cries in my head—a whale breaches, the owl hoots, the turkeys make guttural talk in the yellow grass, and a hand strikes a bold chord and brings me up short—and others look askance at me and grow angry when I vanish into this silent music.

The thunder of the black and ivory as those fingers fly across the keyboard.

Do Good Things

I am facing south but I think it is north. The night is cold, a bad wind off the East River. The woman lights a thin cigarette. She is very pale and comes from one of those peoples of Europe where delicate blue veins snake just below the skin. She is almost translucent and she is careful about drinking too much coffee. She seldom smiles. Her face glows with cold fire, like burning ice. Her hip bones always press against me and that is the sensation, warmth and bones. Her hungers are guarded and then suddenly the leash slips. Her words clipped, almost slurred in the torrent of her feeling, her eyes never resting, scent flooding the air. And I stare south and think I stare north. My sense of direction is gone. I remember that moment in New York and the cold and my failure to know the way home.

During the dinner in the chop house, she takes command. I have no ideas or goals. The editor has no need of them. He simply decides. Editors are to know, not explain. This is when I get my chance at money and oblivion. There is a delay in our seating—he refuses service until placed in the territory of his favored waiter. The walls are dark wood. Everything noise and some cigar smoke. Voices ring out. There is a moment when I am a boy and I sprawl on a wooden floor of a farm house and write on coarse blank sheets with a red crayon, write words and sentences, page after page of greasy language, write about a bolt in the blue, a bird in flight, a man in flight, escape, write with explosive energy that I will later know as desire. So I avoid the city that decides what can be sold. And now I am here. I want the woman with the pale skin. I want to make money. I want to forget the editor after he insists on his waiter. But I wait. I think I can get the money and do good things. My pattern has been simple—bankroll my stories and then sell them. I spend over half of my small income on expenses for the stories. So I sit down and order a thick pork chop and side of steakhouse potatoes. Everything is heavy—the plates, the cutlery, the food.

There is a moment after sunrise on a January morning—thousands of ducks, some geese, a golden eagle, glare off the ice, and that sun rising above the mountains to the east—and in that moment I have no doubt that I am looking at the path that takes me to the stories and sentences and reason for the work. That golden eagle descends, huge wings flapping, veering right to left, seeking a landing.

The ducks lift at my approach on the mudflats. I hear shotguns to the north as hunters shoot from their blinds. Until that moment, I am certain that I am the only human being on Earth. This sensation of cold and light and the sounds of life, the glare off the ice, cranes etched against the sky, thousands of grebes and green-winged teals.

He is sitting on the porch of the white farm house in Wisconsin drinking whiskey as he stares into the green trees of August. His speech is southern and he remembers a war twenty years gone, that second big one. He walks into the empty barracks of the concentration camp, hears a whirring and realizes bodies are racked on the planks of shelving. But they are alive and this is their call. He never really wins his battle with the bottle after that. His voice flows over the summer lawn, a syrup of vowels and drowned passions, and then with dusk the voice moves amid the fireflies.

Another man tells of the last months of that second big one, and he takes out a nest of enemy on a hillside and discovers he has blown away a bunch of fourteen-year-olds. When he tells this story, the cancer is eating him but the moment standing over the warm bodies still remains fresh. He'd never been out of his town before they sent him to Europe to kill. His face is lined and he is a life of mesquite fires. He remembers the summer rains of his desert childhood, the beans and tortillas before first light and always the cutting of the wood to sell.

The ducks and grebes, that golden eagle, they are out on a flat. Voices whisper in my head, a milk wagon rolls down the alley, the horse slump-backed and sweating, the ice melting and dripping out the back, the clink of the bottles, black men briefly safe in the neighborhood as they push wheelbarrows of coal to basement chutes, the ragman shouting, that guy with the sharpening wheel pushing it and chanting as the women pour out of the houses clutching fistfuls of dull knives and on the street three blocks north those tales of the fight on Saturday night where the guy had his ear bit off, bit clean off they say.

The brown pelican dives, then surfaces, the fish in its pouch, a reddish egret dances in the shallows driving prey, two vultures sit on the oyster bed at low tide.

Cranes beating big wings across my eye.

When we leave the chop house in New York, and I think south is north and the woman with pale skin tugs at me and does the talking, the editor suddenly breaks off when a bum comes up, and says, "This is my bum" and gives him some money just as he'd given some money to his waiter that night.

God

The altar in the corner has crepe paper on an old orange crate. I am determined to find God. The apartment window faces a brick wall. I am seven, go to Sunday school, and envy my Catholic friends who wear things around their neck. Their nuns and priests dress as if God exists. My Baptist pastor shouts and acts as if the Devil exists. His two daughters are loose, they say, but I am too young to understand. I want something clean and pure that says I am doing the right thing.

The churches attract me with their good wood, stained glass, choirs and the bug-eyed saints staring off the walls in the cathedrals. The nuns still wear habits and the confessional seems the chamber of mysteries to me. I wait while my Catholic friends confess. I don't think God exists.

There is always this acrid undertone in the homes of old people, a thinness of something missing, churches smell the same way.

The line, the agents, the people hunted on my ground—I did not think of such things when I was decorating that orange crate with crepe.

The altar is tucked away on the east wall of the bedroom I share with my brother. Dark bricks stare at me through the window, I can never see a tree and blue sky. In the late afternoon, light pours in the kitchen window from the west. I want to flee.

The golden eagle on the pole waits out morning stillness. Six turkey hens move into the tall grass. The woman says after the fire on the mountain the bear came down and now raids her bird feeders. Lions move along the creek bottom. The green heron has returned to the pond near the line.

In Louisiana, the tire goes bad. The garage pulls a nail, fixes it for nothing. The man stands there, his pale face above a gut spilling over his belt. A black man about thirty stands by his side.

"Nothing?"

The pale man nods and says, "Well, sumthin' for the boy."

I hand him ten bucks.

A Louisiana heron feeds on the shore under the bald cypress, a brown pelican dives, comes up with a fish in its pouch. The American bittern hides in the cattails, the sky hangs heavy with rain and suddenly a white ibis lands and glows in the dim light. The trees of the rookery are festooned with old nests. The waters host alligators, the wading birds do not nest unless they are safe from raccoons.

I am told don't complain about work, they take forty hours out of your life but leave you the rest. I stare up at the birds twirling around the tiny island. I want all the hours. I want real work.

I sit in the feeble sun of January reading about Nelson Algren. He knew the streets that caged me as a child. Algren has this dream. In that dream, a bunch of writers sit at a long table with Dylan Thomas, and he looks pale because he is dead. Everyone pretends he is alive but they all know he is dead. Thomas turns to Algren and asks, "What did you put in my drink?" Algren has killed him, everyone at the table knows it.

He tells him he's alive.

Dylan says no, he's not alive. He can't write anymore. All he can do is drink.

Common moorhens peck at the wet ground with red bills. A kingfisher waits on the wire. Over there, look, look, a reddish egret dances and drives fish to the surface and its murderous beak.

I want to do something worthy of a dog's love.

> Jesus answered, and said unto him, Art thou a master of Israel, and knowest not these things?

These words, John 3:10, float off a banner draped on the old house facing south toward Mexico. A coffin rests on the front lawn. Paper flowers gaze into the sunlight.

The woods go dark under a moonless sky, the stars shout at me. My old man's been drinking, there is always that, and these storms come without warning. It is part of the sense of otherness—not safe to bring friends home, not safe to think of home—that colors my early life. My memories are dreams of leaving, a child hobo with my bindle on my shoulder heading down a dirt road. Always the light is afternoon and cornfields line the way with crows calling. This never happens but still I remember it. In the end, his drinking is not the important thing, his drinking is simply training for the important thing. Being on the outside. And wanting to stay outside.

There is an afternoon outside of Culiacán at the ranch of a drug dealer. The men sit outside a pigsty on a bench and joke with a *marimacha*, the lesbian who works at the place. The sky is blue, there is the faint tang of ocean, fruit trees flower and the scent rolls over everyone. I know the owner. Once he explained that when he murdered his nephew he had no choice. The scent of orange blossoms lingers, that faint tang of the sea, and the bustling good spirits of the lesbian working at the pigsty on a sunny afternoon.

I want to stop.

I want the authorities to know this and show mercy.

There is a man sliding down the slope, he is the alien and he is the enemy. I want to join him.

So too, the birds, the bears, lions, bugs, wild seeds from errant flowers, the creek rising, owl hunting in the blackness, all the outsiders. We will all ride in the night and fire will flame out of the nostrils of our steeds and we will throw fear into the nations.

I meet an old priest. In the days of the dictatorship in Chile, he would stand in front of the government building for four minutes holding a sign denouncing the torture. The police took five minutes to arrive. Eventually, he was expelled.

Now he is a frail old man. His hands feel tiny, his body something made of gossamer. There is a brogue in his voice.

The room is mainly old men and women, nuns and priests. They have lived with the poor. They speak of other nations the way I know neighborhoods.

The old priests and nuns, they have remained fools for life. They gather in a house dedicated to St. Columbanus, a mad Irish monk who sought to live alone in the woods. Birds alighted on his tunic, squirrels ran down trees to nestle in his cowl. He was obsessed with the proper date for Easter. On the walls are the faces of martyrs, nuns, slaughtered in the Central American wars.

I stare around the meeting house, the old nuns and priests on chairs, their eyes alert, their faces happy. They have the bearing of lives spent but not squandered.

The Mexican jays come to the feeder, acorn woodpeckers drive them away.

The nuns and priests listen closely to the tale of a killer who could have been something professional, a man with a good career, if he'd only been born five thousand yards north of his barrio and on this side of a line. They quietly nod. They have been to the wars I skipped. They are further down the path than me.

They are old, their tribe seems to be dying out after fifteen centuries. None of it, the martyrs, the wars, the wicked, the face of evil, the blood that is wine and the bread that is flesh, the endless rows of nameless graves where saints are poured from their sackcloth into the cold yet hungry earth and Matthew says

> For I was an hungred, and ye gave me meat: I was thirsty, and ye gave me drink: I was a stranger, and ye took me in.

and none of them and none of the centuries they wandered and none of their suffering was wasted, not a minute, because what matters is not about winning but about love and the gospel according to Matthew goes

> Naked, and ye clothed me: I was sick, and ye visited me: I was in prison, and ye came unto me.

and two javelina cross the dirt road, the pickup truck never slows, the driver never gives them a glance, black-throated sparrows move through the thicket, their faces a painted mask in white and black,

> Then shall the righteous answer him, saying, Lord, when saw we thee an hungred, and fed thee? or thirsty, and gave thee drink?

I hear cranes but I cannot see them, they are south, past the barrier on into Mexico. The field in front of me is brown, leaves spent, red chili hanging. About a hundred men and women move down the rows. Sacks stuffed with chili wait by the road. The people are bent, the sky blue. Across the barrier is the village that has hurled labor into these fields for generations without the sanction of law but with the desire of the growers. At a pond, ducks explode into the air and veer south

> When saw we thee a stranger, and took thee in? or naked, and clothed thee?
>
> Or when saw we thee sick, or in prison, and came unto thee?

and before the women got bad, before I succumbed to long nights and motel beds, I met a nun. She was young, in her late twenties, and she was at an old church in a barrio. The neighborhood was dirt dreams. The young men dreamed of being prizefighters. The young women dreamed of the young men. Women in the barrio held a vigil each year for the Virgin and the women prayed while the men drank and tended the fire. There was menudo for all.

I remember telling a friend, an old border hand, of the woman.

He snorted, "She's got a foul mouth, she was a whore in Guadalajara."

The nun takes me through the church—hard pews, dust and old wood. The people of the barrio built it. The three priests each totter on ninety. They share about two centuries of service to their God and now they end it here. A block down the street women sell themselves. The barber has a photo album of them going back decades, images culled from when they rest in his chairs between clients. The three priests spin out their life here.

I am having a drink. This time the woman is scent and warm smiles.

I tell her of the old priests and the church. I do not mention the young nun because I think that will distract the woman. I say the old priests in an old building in a poor barrio accomplish more than the people I read about in the newspapers or hear giving speeches.

She says she had her first communion at that church and she can tell me all about priests. They have more than religion on their minds she says.

She is not smiling now.

I remember that photograph album the barber kept of the whores that worked the street outside the church. One of them had a son serving in a war, I can't remember which one. So nothing is as simple as I desire. In some of the photographs the women are nodding off from their fix of heroin. In some, they expose parts of their body. The barber fences things on the side.

Do the right thing.

Be the enemy.

> For I was an hungred, and ye gave me no meat: I was thirsty, and ye gave me no drink:
>
> I was a stranger, and ye took me not in: naked, and ye clothed me not: sick, and in prison, and ye visited me not.

He slides down the slope, he is dirty and hungry and illegal.

At the bar, a Border Patrol agent tells me that they take down loads all the time, every day. The Mexicans never shoot when caught on this side. It is part of the business, these losses. South of us, just across that line, four dead men come out of the sewage pond in the village where the work is smuggling drugs. Two are wrapped in blankets, two stuffed in barrels.

A Cooper's hawk hunts the creek, birds flee my feeders.

> Then shall they also answer him, saying, Lord, when saw we thee an hungred, or athirst, or a stranger, or naked, or sick, or in prison, and did not minister unto thee?

The nuns and priests sit in rows. They have crossed the line and this has made them at times the enemy.

There is a place near the creek where an owl roosts in the heart of a hackberry tree during the day. At night, the owl hunts. Once, I spooked the owl around noontime and it flew off into the glare of light. Now I avoid the place when the owl rests from its night of murders.

And the man slides down the slope, comes out of the tall grass, tired, dirty, brown and against the law.

Goya

The small dog rises from a slope of brown on the wall of the house of demons just outside Madrid where Goya lived as an old man. There is some debate about whether Goya made the paintings. But there is no debate about what was found on the walls. The small dog's head looks black, the eye gleams.

The black dog came long before Goya. Some scholars trace the beast back to the Viking raids. They had tales of the hellhound that accompanied the Norse god Odin. Winston Churchill was one of many to call his depression the black dog.

In a house outside Madrid someone painted the dog on the wall of his home. Someone also painted a god eating his children.

Almost the earliest surviving lines of Anglo-Saxon poetry go:

The masonry is wondrous; fates broke it.
    The courtyard pavements were smashed;
    The work of giants is decaying.

Stars fall out of the sky.
    Love stumbles.
    The lion pads down the trail.

In the gray light, two wild turkeys cross the road and leave spidery tracks.

As a child I race through the corn, the stalks towering over me, the leaves making fine thin slices on my flesh.

The French execute the Spaniards before the walls of Madrid and Francisco Goya draws.

Guernica goes down from bombs on April 26, 1937. By June, Picasso's huge painting looks out at the world.

A meteor shower scratches the night.

At dusk, a great blue heron fishes the dark waters of the creek.

There is a painting by George Inness where the heron can hardly be found in the murk of a day ending. He painted it when he was an old man and could hardly see. There is a painting by George Inness that was commissioned by a railroad, and a train crosses the Lackawanna Valley, in the background looms the roundhouse, stumps of murdered trees dot the land. One of the founders of American landscape painting, by the time he painted his heron in the failing light, he did not leave his studio. He found the American landscape he loved in his memory and he stayed there where it was safe.

In 1894, he watches the sunset in New Jersey and shouts, "My God, oh, how beautiful."

Then, he falls dead to the ground.

The Asylum

A friend sends me a photograph of a man in an insane asylum in Ciudad Juárez. The man holds a baseball cap that announces WALK BY FAITH. A note is attached to the image. The cook at the asylum says the man killed fifteen people. The head of the asylum, a minister, says, no, no, it was many more than that but it does not matter, the man has repented.

I look up and see a great blue heron moving past with that slow wing beat.

There is this noise in my head that will not stop.

He leaves. He returns. He says little or nothing of the journey. Or why he left. There is a time he hits a bridge. Once he mentions seeing *Hamlet* in Little Rock.

He eats out of cans, heats food on a small stove in the truck. The VW bus gives way to the half-ton pickup, then comes the bread van he retrofitted with bunk, stove and storage.

There is no schedule to his travels. He goes. He returns.

He never says he is looking for something. He never says he found something.

I am his son.

Now I leave and come back.

There are lion tracks by the creek.

I report nothing.

The sun comes up, the red truck is in the drive and then

later in the day it is gone and nothing is said. His face always grizzled with a two-day beard, the truck rumbling, instant coffee, canned beans, chicken and potatoes in the larder, half a dozen cases of beer and a bottle of gin, he'd be off, highways picked at random. On the engine housing by the driver, carpeting glued to give a grip for bottles, ashtrays and other tools.

He sits, smoke curling off his hand-rolled cigarette. He sits, gin swirling in his coffee cup. He sits, a tattered paperback in his hand. Sometimes he tunes in the radio for a burst of news. He will sit for days on desert hillsides under a tree reading and drinking. The coasts are fine also, the truck door open, a sea breeze and ten miles to the nearest town. The middle south is green and that can be good. Nevada has blackjack, poker and roulette. Utah has been scratched from the list, too many rules on drink. Always, there is Mexico, a place where the hungry nights of his childhood still live on the faces.

Go.

I am his son.

Rise, drink black coffee, check out of the motel.

Rise drink black coffee, roll up the sleeping bag.

Rise, drink black coffee, never move for days, the notebook blank pages.

There is never enough but always enough, the sanctuary is not in another country but in this country, a country without name or location, the country under my feet that has the bones of my ancestors and will hold my bones, a country in my bones. I am a boy on the marsh, cattails brown and water frozen at the edge, the sound of ducks, green teal blazing on the gray, there is no Eden, there never was an Eden, we are in Eden and must face this fact. The highways are lies.

In the yard at the asylum the crazy people line up against a winter wall, the one with the gray beard wears a green tinfoil hat and unsmiling eyes, the pigs stare from the pens, their bodies lean, there has been no food, last week five men died, one-two-three-four-five, the men sweep litter in the yard, feed chickens, stack chairs, a fire glows in the kitchen and people surround it, in the sky black crows against slate gray, wood smoke bites the air, a woman comes up, small, a gnome, her head in a hood and a toothless smile and I lean now and kiss her, turkeys roasted with peas and carrots spilling out as dressing, and Christ is born they say far away long ago, that is the talk, Christmas day. A man slips down a slope, comes out of the tall grass and asks which way is Atlanta and I must answer.

The Fifth Sun

The First Sun is the time when wild animals destroyed the world. The Second Sun brought the wind, the Third fire. Then come the floods of the Fourth Sun. But the Fifth Sun takes everything down with motion, the ground-shaking ruin and people becoming animals again.

The ancient people of Mexico dread the Fifth Sun.

The motion comes.

Drones fly the Mexican border with their bulbous head, blue band, various radar snouts searching. One comes over the hill, the leaves rustle on the live oaks, the craft moving almost silently, skimming as it hunts for the enemies of the state.

The air feels fresh from the rain, the drone almost purrs as it rolls over the hill and plunges down into the hunt.

> And it shall come to pass, that when they make a long blast with the ram's horn, and when ye hear the sound of the trumpet, all the people shall shout with a great shout; and the wall of the city shall fall down flat, and the people shall ascend up every man straight before him.

* * *

The city hangs across the freeway in the dust. The houses, rutted lanes and broken cars make a tapestry on a hillside of dirt. There was a day when someone rolled a couch across the road by the river. When a car stopped, they robbed it and waded back.

The gallery is now open. Red lights dangle in the antechamber. Photographs line the wall.

The images record where the whores slowly wasted away with drugs, disease and that occasional murderous trick.

Now that the buildings are rubble, the world of these women can be considered.

Now it is washed clean of pain.

* * *

There is the man with no feet. He struggles now. He tries to work in a fast-food place but it is too much. Phantom pains plague his severed limbs. He had a business and employees. He supplied the food and snacks at public events. But that was before the incident, he likes to refer to it as the incident. He has fled across the river and after a while he will vanish from memory.

It went like this. They come and throw him down. The boss watches. One man is on his chest facing him. Another holds his arms down. Someone cuts but he is not sure how—an ax? a saw? He can't be sure. The man telling me this account pauses when he remembers working in a chicken factory and how hard it was to cut through the bones.

Another story. A man leaves a small town I favor. He must go over there on a business matter and he is told not to bring his phone. No one hears from him and he does not come back.

Another story. A friend tells me he no longer knows who to call when the bad things happen and so he has no hope of fixing it or saving himself. In town on the big highway, the police change. Before they worked with criminals. To be outside the law, the law had to be paid. Now, the law works with them. Then, the next phase arrives. You are out to eat with your wife and a man walks up to your table and says I want to fuck your wife, have her at my house at eight p.m.

Clouds lift, sun pours through blue sky, five crows dive at a Cooper's hawk on the treetop.

A man tells me that man with no feet is now "a total ruin." He looks down and his fork toys with the quiche on his plate. Crows caw overhead on the patio, the wall is brown stucco with blue trim.

When Tenochtitlan falls, Cortes stands on a surviving rooftop amid the rubble of the Indian world. He has Cuauhtémoc brought to him and promises he will be fine, so too his wife, the daughter of the late Montezuma, and he will again rule his world. This lie is intended to soothe him before he is tortured. The conquistadors notice the silence. No more sound of drums, whistles, horns, conch shells, screams and shouts. Thunder, the rain falls. Spaniards walk around the murdered city holding white kerchiefs to their noses to block the stench off the corpses.

The Cooper's hawk does not return. The crows move off.

The beginning has the feel of a dream. The sky fills with a tongue of fire. The thatched room atop a pyramid burns. The lake foams. There is a flood. This is before the strangers appear.

To the east in the islands, Ponce De Leon keeps a dog, Becerrillo, Little Calf, and the dog casts terror into the native people in Puerto Rico. He has red hair, black eyes and by scent sorts enemies from friends. His son, Leoncillo, Little Lion, is with Balboa in Panama.

The dying comes. One chief run to ground in Cuba is offered death by fire if he refuses baptism. Or death by the sword if he converts. He learns if he converts he will spend eternity with the strangers. He chooses the fire. When the fleet casts anchor off Cuba in February 1518, the ships bring mastiffs and Irish wolfhounds. A man close to the leader for the crucial next eighteen months says of him, a man called Hernan Cortes, "he had no more conscience than a dog."

Near a place now called Veracruz, the strangers learn of an empire to the west. Local people send the feathers of roseate spoonbills as tribute. The strangers are stunned by the bird life. A large brown bird dives into the sea and then emerges with a live fish inside its mouth. This they notice. They keep asking about gold.

The world melts, walls fall down, diseases fly to new flesh, bloods mingle. Juan Garrido, a black man out of Africa, a man made Christian in Lisbon, comes with the fleet. He plants the first wheat in Mexico.

The emperor gets messages.

There is an ashen crane with a mirror in its head. He stares and sees the stars, the heavens and men of war riding deer. He calls for other men, wise men, to look into the mirror. But when they arrive, that bird has flown.

The staccato voice taps against the still morning air.

The man from the east causes some worry for the emperor. His arrival has been predicted for years and the emperor worries he is a timeserver to be toppled when the rightful owner returns.

He fears change.

He fears what he has done might be done to him.

He fears.

I take him home. Feed him. Let him shower. Give him my phone so he can make calls to kin scattered across the United States.

I heat up some etouffee, and he devours plate after plate. The roux glows with crushed tomatoes and orange bell peppers. Dots of celery float among the shrimp.

He eats mechanically. The hunger is deep in his body.

I look at the short brown man eating at the long wooden table with Saltillo tiles glowing under his tired feet. He shows me the holes in his socks—I give him a fresh pair. He comes out of the shower with no shirt, I suspect so I can see he has no gang tattoos.

If he heads toward Atlanta, I tell him, he's got fifteen hundred miles to go. Los Angles means six hundred or so.

He is unworried. Mexico was rough—they rob and kill Central American migrants there. His home, San Pedro Sula, is sometimes listed as the most violent place in the western hemisphere.

He just wants to work, he explains, he is not fleeing the violence.

He has no record. He is clean, he says. He carries no identification. He can invent his identity if captured by *la migra*. He came alone. He has no money.

Which way is Atlanta?

He hears rumors. He studies faces. He looks closely at gifts for glints of gold and silver. The men have been told never to dismount from their horses lest a mystery be revealed. When his scouts first see Cempoallan, the sun dances on the white rooftops and they think them made of silver. The headman sends out turkeys for the strangers and explains he cannot come because he is too fat to move. This is taken as a sign that they are entering a rich country.

Five captives in the town are soon to be sacrificed. He seizes them to prevent the slaughter. But the headman protests: "You will ruin me and all this kingdom if you rob me of these slaves. Our infuriated gods will send locusts to devour our harvests, hail to beat them down, drought to burn them, and torrential rain to swamp them if we offer no more sacrifices." The priests with the strangers argue it is the wrong moment to end human sacrifice. The slaves are returned to their deaths.

> The banner says, Thousands of assassinations, executions, decapitations without any resolution.
>
> The banner displays a skull and crossbones floating under the word Chihuahua.

The sun warms Juárez on a Saturday afternoon. The morning glories are still open, chickens peck at the hard ground. Names cover the patio wall. She and the priest keep a list of the dead and she asks each visitor to write a few on the wall. There are thousands still to record. The beans are up, so are the radishes and broccoli.

At lunch, they say grace, pour wine. The sister leans forward on the kitchen table and remembers when they trained a refugee from Guatemala so that *la migra*, the agents, would not spot her at the airport and ship her back to the slaughter. Then one of the nuns drove her to the airport, repeating that she was not to speak to her there or make any sign they knew each other.

The nun sat in the corner of the waiting room.

Finally, boarding began. The Indian woman made it out the gate and to the staircase leading up to the plane.

Then she paused and carefully balanced the suitcase on her head.

The nun looks up from her kitchen table. "That was all it took."

The agents pounced.

Buses pass here each day, no writing on them, painted white, the windows covered with convict screen, and they hum toward the border where the cargos are kicked back over the line. Or they hum down the highway to private prisons.

No one pays much attention.

At the south end of the valley a Mexican takes a round in the thigh that severs his femoral artery. He dies. The authorities say bandits did the killing.

I saw my first loggerhead strike in this valley, the last wolf run in the region nicked its corner up by the Canelo hills. They killed the pups, the bitch fled back into Mexico. Apaches coursed south through this green smear to raid south and there is a monument to Spaniards coming north. They find the body next to this memorial.

A lookout for a load coming north, one escorted by the Mexican army, sees the Border Patrol shoot the Mexican.

That is what they say on the other side of the fence.

Here there is an official version and it is not questioned.

Then, silence returns to the grassland.

I look at the Honduran. He is still using my phone to call relatives scattered in the shadows around the United States. He talks endlessly with an aunt and his voice is soft and tender.

I thought this matter would be very hard.

I was wrong.

The bus goes by with screens on the windows.

The people speak out against being killed about the time the bank swallows migrate along the river. They stand in front of the Mexican consulate as sun seeps through the trees along the sidewalk. Signs with photographs of vanished brothers and sisters and mothers and fathers stare out as the city hums around them. The signs glow red, green, yellow and white in the shade. Four television cameras line up to face the group of thirty. People speak one by one.

Cars slide past. The killing field begins a few hundred yards to the south.

The man sitting on the sofa says the whole thing was their idea. They wanted to have a protest in front of the consulate of the nation that had killed the people they loved and threatened to kill them. He dabs at his lips as he speaks, he moistens his gums, also. The radiation and chemotherapy have dried up his mouth. For a while he could not speak. Eating remains a problem. He has lost forty pounds.

The people standing outside the consulate seek political asylum. He is their lawyer.

He talks of small places and says, "I think Guadalupe and Villa Ahumada are the new model. They come now and kill you and take your property and this is never reported. In Villa Ahumada five people were killed and it was never reported. When that family of twenty-two came over together to save their lives, I think that was the largest such flight by a family since the revolution."

He dabs at his dry gums.

He says in one town the chief of police always calls the head of the organization before he makes an arrest. He says if something bad happens to you in that town there is no one to call. He says this is the future he sees unfolding.

He dabs his gums again.

The man stands over the table. He is tall and old and has a paunch. He patrols the border at times in order to keep people from crossing illegally. He does this out of a sense of duty. The wall snakes just to the south, ten, fifteen feet high in this section with bars so agents can see through it and shoot and kill anyone who throws rocks at them. There is a hole near the fence full of brown water. No bird comes.

The man says the agents should park all along the border and then no one would come north in the day or the night. The man says the woman came out of some bar and then they took her and she has not been seen since. She'd been warned by her competitors, he notes, to stop selling drugs and she did not obey.

Fifteen years ago, he charged $650 to move people from the fence to a town forty miles north. For more money, he would drive a rented truckload to Denver. He could make seven grand, he says, in eight hours.

He looks up from his plate of beans and beef and advises, "Fast as you make it, you spend it. I'd see somebody who needed clothes, I'd take him to a store and fix him up. Once I paid a friend $700 just to ride along for company on the drive to Denver. You spend it fast."

At dawn the sky is clear, a light breeze stirring the leaves on the tree. The water a flat plate of silver with thousands of cranes. First, eight white pelicans swing into view, then a pod of forty floats off on the edge of a pond, then a group of a hundred.

He says he would back right up to the fence to load them, then drive forty miles to a stash house and after that make the calls and get more money and take them further north. He had people watching checkpoints and they'd call in when they were open and when they were closed. Sometimes, the agents would be a problem. He'd pay Mexican kids to throw rocks at them and keep them busy while he loaded his truck up somewhere else along the line.

He didn't use any drugs, you need a clear head for this kind of work. But he was good to the people he moved. He'd put a bucket of ice in the back of the rental truck before he locked them in. And he'd let them go to the bathroom then because once he started to roll they were to stay out of sight until he made it to his destination.

Then, that girl died. She was young, they didn't give her water. She had to walk from the line to the pickup point. She didn't make it. She was not in his group. Still that brought trouble. The boss who controlled that crossing was toppled and there was a big fight among the groups over who would be the new boss.

He worked for a real tough lady, actually her whole family was in the business, and she said to go away for a while until things settled down. So he did. But he never came back.

Prison got in the way, something about drugs, and then he got out and now he's clean and has a different life. He was born Mexican but now he's US.

He laughs over his plate of beans and beef at the memories.

He calls the passengers in the back of his rented truck cargo, worth so much a head.

That's how it all gets done.

Later, the big wind comes, fifty or sixty miles an hour. The sky turns brown with dust. The ducks hide in the reeds, the pelicans drift off into elbows of the water that are sheltered from the wind.

Crossing the Line

I feel the wood. Out on the water they fish for bass. The bar is rosewood and the glow off the varnish colors the room. The place seats 200, the horseshoe bar offers more stools.

No one comes here.

I order a red wine.

She asks, "Do you want that hot or cold?"

She finds a bottle and tries to unscrew.

"You need a corkscrew."

She looks up, nods.

I drink.

No one comes here.

There is construction outside for the addition to the place no one comes.

Six blocks away is the sheriff's office. He says violence is spilling across the line. In a cove below the bar, a man stands in a small skiff and casts. A woman tells me people she has known for years who are scratching out a living herding goats suddenly move to town and build big houses.

In the Ravensbrück concentration camp, Elsa Krug, a prostitute who specialized in masochistic clients, was told to beat another inmate. She refused. So they executed her.

The wine is neither hot nor cold.

Decades ago, I picked up people in the desert and drove them to ranches and farms where they worked. They did not speak English and they were very hot and tired.

Would you like the wine hot or cold?

The seized load is reported as 800 pounds. The load taken down is actually 3000 pounds.

Years ago, I knew of a load of sixty kilos of cocaine seized by agents and never reported.

I asked an official about this.

He said, "We know we have a problem."

* * *

The coffin in the front yard says it is for Elias, Rueben, Josefina, and Malena Reyes. Their mother sits on the sidewalk in a folding chair.

A banner says they live in Chihuahua with fear, corruption, apathetic government.

The mother's face is stern.

* * *

There are over forty photographs of the dead or near dead. One woman has been missing eighteen months, but her son puts her photograph to the side of the altar because he wishes to think of her as still alive. The little signs tell stories: "assassinated October 30 2006." There is a woman marching with a huge photograph of her murdered daughter plastered to her body. The woman also was murdered. The sun warms the earth, the faces do not smile.

He sits at the long table, skin brown, moustache a faint shadow over his lip. The shirt a light green, the pants blue black and almost falling off him. That month crossing Mexico, three days without food before he stumbled out of the brush and into my life.

There are a few seconds in the gathering dusk when I pretend not to see him because I don't want to deal with his needs or deal with the laws or deal with anything beyond myself.

He becomes the other, someone that can be denied. The way that roadkill flickers as the eyes flash in the headlights and the animal vanishes under the wheels and then the car speeds on as if it never happened.

There was that day a few years back when the agents swept town and twenty-odd people vanished. No one talked about them. They'd broken the law. She worked part time in the local café, her eye always gleaming and never focused.

She smiled a lot, never buttoned the top of her blouse and leaned forward when she put down the plates.

Once I asked where the rich lived in town and she looked puzzled.

She said, twirling her hands, "It's all mixed up here, all mixed up."

In the late afternoon, she'd come out of the tiny grocery with her boyfriend and a twelve-pack. Then he got mad one day and tried to strangle her. The café put up a hand-lettered sign how nobody could talk bad there.

After the bust, the café changed hands. The agents said they'd taken down a major ring.

Then silence, as if she had never existed.

He drops down the slope, out of the brush and for that second, I decide he does not exist because then I will not have to deal with him.

But it is too late.

The man drops down the slope, out of the brush and onto the dirt road, for that second, I decide not to see him, to continue looking at a gray hawk on the cottonwood tree by the creek. They are rare.

In the long ago, I am on a faltering river. The man sets up mist nets for capturing and banding gray hawks. I wander the woods, find small shelters made of sticks where woodcutters hide from the law. They come up from Mexico, cut mesquite, then take their wages and drift back south again. Finally, a study shows the woodcutting changes the world of the gray hawk and holds their numbers down. The saws cease, the nestlings increase.

I hold a quivering gray hawk, heat rises from its body.

Thirteen were banded in Mexico, eleven of them were shot.

I turn toward him.

She tells me the house will go. She has seen big water and it will come again and then the place by the creek will be gone, torn from its foundation by the flood.

"Yes," she says, smacking her thin lips, "it can't last. I raised five boys just up the canyon. I know what that creek can do."

The car rolls past, dust rises in my face, I see her face framed by sunglasses. The thin tube leads from the oxygen bottle to her nose. She is going to the bar.

I enter the bar. She sits there with her beer and oxygen bottle.

The waters will rise.

Mother

She knits with her arthritic fingers, that clacking of the needles, sometimes she embroiders. She can watch television and do those things. But crocheting, the single hook, seems to spear the moment and become everything.

Her mother's mother left a tablecloth that is kept in the lower drawers of a china cabinet and that sees the light of day at Thanksgiving and Christmas, the same times small silver salt and pepper shakers emerge.

The tablecloth holds dead hands in the knots, the stabbing of the hook, long evenings on the plains with snow piling up and blocking first-story windows, a line strung to the barn for the storms, the tales of people lost in whiteouts, cars that pull over and the bodies stiff as rocks, the cattle sheltering in a draw, the endless nights, bleak light at noon, sky as hard as an anvil, the hook jabbing up, she leans forward, evening coming, a china cup and saucer with weak coffee by her side, and a white lace pattern of hard knots spilling onto her lap, the eyes focused behind her glasses, and there is a row of skulls, there atop the temple, racks of skulls, all from the sacrificed, slaves, warriors, girls, women, children, all chests ripped open, limbs severed, cooked and seasoned with chili, the skulls remembering those who gave their lives so the rains would come, the sun rise, the crops thrive, the gods be kind, racks of skulls, and in the plains the snows come and she leans forward, crochet hook stabbing, the towns falling into ruin, farmsteads collapsing, headstones tilting at the cemetery, bodies stacked until the ground thaws in the spring, the smell of raw earth when the soil finally comes back, tulips poking through the last snow, the sermon in the church, dirt hitting the coffin lid, sky gray on the burying days, ducks and geese in Vs heading north as the men and women troop back from the graveyard, the women on the streets of the city have tattoos and this stuns the strangers, the old records say

> she parades, she moves lasciviously . . . she appears like a flower, looks gaudy . . . views herself in a mirror . . . she bathes . . . she goes about with her head high . . . rude, drunk, shameless, eating mushrooms. She paints her face, variously paints her face, her face is covered with rouge, her cheeks are colored . . . rubbed with cochineal . . . she arranges her hair like horns . . . finds pleasure in her body . . .

the stab of the crochet hook, the knots to tie generations together as they eat a hundred years of holiday meals on the lacy cloth, racks of skulls, the priests with blood-clotted dreadlocks, bodies tossed down the steep steps of the pyramids, and after the thaw in the spring lilacs bloom by the door, the lowing of the cattle, the white snow of apple blossoms come spring.

Great blue herons line the river, one, two, three, four, five. A harrier stoops, a kestrel feeds on a telephone pole.

She sits in the afternoon light with her hook.

The mountains say nothing. The stone tablets lie broken, the burning bush gives no heat. The tongues have been ripped from the living earth.

The deserts and the ocean cease speaking.

The gods are silent, also.

A woman prays in a café over a plate of cheap food.

A man chokes up as he explains he cannot feed his children.

Then silence.

Crossing the Line

He unfolds the small map, one torn from a child's schoolbook. Mexico is there, a fringe of little nations on its south, a band of the United States just past the Rio Grande.

He looks up and asks again where is Atlanta. I point, he follows my finger.

A cardinal bathes in the creek where the clear water runs over the rocks. The red body bobs and shakes and bobs again.

He unfolds a white piece of paper with twenty or thirty phone numbers and names neatly inscribed. Family. I hand him my phone. He calls a relative in Atlanta.

I spread out maps. I show routes. I mark checkpoints. I tell him agents are everywhere.

He nods.

He says he feels safe.

Mexico, that was dangerous, he says.

That time in Nuevo Laredo, the Central Americans came out from the shadows like hunted animals and begged for food. When I handed over some pesos, they ran a block to a taco cart. All this in front of the shelter for migrants, one with locked doors. A man walks up. His arm is bent between his elbow and his wrist. He fell from a boxcar coming up from Central America, fell off the line called the train of death where Mexicans lasso travelers riding on the top of boxcars. He set the arm himself. He's going to cross that river, he wants to work.

The man from Honduras is calm. He has spent a month getting through Mexico. He has eaten. He has showered.

The maps, the maps are just drawings of the ground and he has crossed day after day of ground. He paints houses. He works. The ground that must be covered, that is nothing.

He looks at the map as I mark the checkpoint.

* * *

The air conditioner in the cab is never turned on. The temperature rides a hundred ten, sometimes bumps a hundred twenty. It is forty miles or more with no water. Belts of dunes block routes.

The agent drinks hot coffee.

The day begins after first light when footprints are heightened by shadow.

In the heat of summer, the heat kills and no one ever learns how many go down.

The radio crackles. Six have left tracks near the line. He roars down a parallel road and finds they have crossed, heads north, and goes down another path.

I remember the hunt and wanting to catch the prey.

In the cab bouncing along the desert track it feels like a game.

* * *

The paper flowers are yellow and orange and red and blue and they smile near the coffin in the front yard of the old house. The television cameras line up. A table and chairs are brought out and one by one speakers tell of murders and pain and fear and corruption and the lack of justice. A tall Aleppo pine casts shade to one side.

The old woman whose children's names stare up from the coffin never smiles. Or wavers.

The sun beats down but she is more relentless than the sun.

* * *

After the surgery, they roll him into the intensive care unit. He has never been a patient since they locked him in the pest house as a boy.

They cut him bad at the throat and part of his mouth. He can't talk clearly after going under the knife. He never will again. I spend the night by his bed, the life-support machines whirring away.

When he is discharged a few days later, the hospital insists he use a wheelchair.

As soon as he clears the hospital door, he stands and walks away. Once home, he sits at his kitchen table and rolls a cigarette. He inhales deeply, blue smoke floats up to the high ceiling in the old house.

He turns on the radio, catches the market report.

He ignores me.

When he was a young buck, he dug ditches, shucked corn, stacked shocks of wheat. Never knocked his father to the ground. The other sons could not make that claim. He was landless. His father drank and doubted the idea of work.

There will be no treatments. He will not waste his time that way. There will be no painkillers, he will not waste his mind that way.

He savors his smoke.

When I was twelve I knocked my father to the ground, the man now snuffing out that cigarette.

The Cranes

I get up and bolt for the door, and onto the highway. The world of cranes beckons. They migrate, they live in various realms, they are ancient in lineage and they bring everything with them, dragging it down a highway millions of years old. The male calls, the female calls, the unison song, voice playing off voice.

Cranes call in my head.

There is a moment in the afternoon light. A great blue heron stands on the edge of a ditch, the long legs of a bullfrog dangle from its bill. The bird twice leans forward and swishes the frog in the water. Then the head tilts back, the bill opens, the frog slides into the gullet and is gone.

Thousands fly overhead on an arc from Siberia and Canada into the south of the US and into Mexico, round trips that can reach 12,000 miles.

The heron clutches the bullfrog in its bill, swishes it back and forth in the water, a man slides out of the tall grass into the fading light and asks which way is Atlanta and I want to not see him and I want to have everything move fast and be gone and now he is there, frozen like the heron, the man, the fading light, the gallon of water on the black pole, his brown and worn and hungry face and I hear the cranes calling across ten million years.

A blue bird explodes out of my forehead. I lean over a spring on the hillside of oak and ash, the mosquitoes so thick I inhale them in the twilight. I can smell potatoes frying in the trailer up the hill, soon to be joined by the sizzle of a cheap steak in the pan, the lantern casting light. Suddenly a blue bird glows before my eyes, an indigo bunting.

The fen gleams green in the Chihuahuan desert. Four canvasbacks float on the nearby pond. The air is the sound of a thousand sandhill cranes. An American bittern lifts from the bed of reeds and then vanishes again, a great horned owl hides in the shade of a willow.

Two couples stand across from the small marsh. Yellow-headed black birds lift up, hover over the bed of reeds like a school of fish and then descend again into their sanctuary. The men throw stones, the wives squeal with delight.

I want to kill them.

Mountains spread blue to the west, the cranes call. For sixty million years cranes have etched their lives on this planet. The early people see them vanish on their migrations and think they must fly through the skies to the gods.

The men are throwing rocks.

The heron is stone calm.

A blue bird explodes in my head.

I want to kill them.

I cross a line. A man slides down the slope, comes out of the grass with his water jug and hunger. The great blue heron stands in brown water, the legs of a bullfrog dangling from its bill. Orion rides in the western sky near dawn, Venus burns a little to the north.

The man slides down the slope—a fugitive from a bad place, a crime as he walks out on the road. I pretend not to see him, pretend for just a second but still pretend and then I cannot keep up this lie and I look at him, hungry, dirty, worn and illegal.

I cross that line.

Crossing the Line

He goes out at night to buy heroin for his mother. That way he does not worry about her getting hurt. Now, she is dead and he is thinking of becoming an agent enforcing drug laws.

The flower girl almost skips down the aisle scattering petals.

Today, he marries.

The bridesmaids wear champagne-colored dresses.

The priest says, "Bone of my bone, flesh of my flesh."

The priest hails from Ciudad Juárez, he reads from Paul's letter to the Corinthians.

He says, "Without love, there is nothing."

Candles burn. The church is full of the sounds of babies.

Outside the sun falls on old graves.

The sister is taken, raped and murdered. Her killer confesses. The court releases the killer. The mother protests. She is executed in front of the governor's palace, the event recorded by surveillance cameras. There are many witnesses. No one is arrested.

The son sits at the table in the windowless room after the press conference.

He is bitter.

"These people don't give a damn for my family. It's not

my priority to convince them. It's my priority for the truth to come out."

He wears a black Batman t-shirt and slumps in his chair. He has come to El Paso from a distant city for this press conference. In El Paso, he always watches his back. People can get snatched and taken across the river to Juárez.

"I am tired of lies. If I were in Mexico, I would be dead. I love my country but I want to live."

He has filed for political asylum in the United States. If he gets it, he will buy a house and work and settle in with his wife and children. His nine-year-old daughter is having problems. She rebels. She asks why was my grandmother murdered? Why was my aunt murdered? He has no answers.

Now he is a waiter. He plays guitar to relax. He was a heroin addict, but life changed him and now there is no room for heroin.

For a year or more, each morning he would wake up and instantly feel the weight of his mother's murder and his sister's murder. This passed.

Now he has become his mother.

Each afternoon after his sister's murder, he would go by his mother's house and she would be crying. Then she would stand up, take her placard with her daughter's picture on it and go down to the government offices and demand justice. When she was slaughtered in front of the governor's palace she was there with her placard.

She died, he thinks, because she spoke of the links between the Mexican government and the drug people.

His mother got up every day.

He says, "You have to get up."

The film rolls of his mother's execution and a contract killer goes over the tape again and again to show me how it was done and the various individuals on the tape who were part of the killing. The woman runs, a man chases her through all the people and cars in front of the capital building. And guns her down. A car pulls up, he gets in, and vanishes. The dead woman's brother sees the killing and identifies the killer and is ignored by the authorities.

Now the son has to get up every day.

His mother expects it.

I sit at a table with some Border Patrol agents. The talk is of the problems of the line. Right now, there is a simple problem: there are many agents and there are not enough Mexicans. The agents do not even average a Mexican each per month. They laugh at what might happen if the public knew.

They can keep the numbers down when they wish.

The agent says, "They'll send you to a place—a hill, a canyon—where people have never walked. They'll keep you there a month. The numbers of captures will go down to almost nothing. And that proves the new policy works."

Wood storks and roseate spoonbills swirl against the gray sky over the green marsh. A mother raccoon and her young break out of the grass and amble past my boot. The air heavy, the heat suffocating. The rain draws near, the bog belches gases, the birds swirl over my head, the wing beats slow.

A pilated woodpecker drums.

The man on the couch leans forward, dabs at his gums.

There is the matter of the man with no feet.

But first, the man with the cancer dabs at his gums and says, "What I want, well, everyone seems to distrust each other but they are all coming from the same experience, and I want them to learn that their pain is not unique, that we must do something together."

There's a pile of books on the coffee table about the concentration camps and the extermination camps.

He dabs that dry gum and continues, "What they want is justice. And that their families not be forgotten."

He sinks back onto the couch.

The Asylum

The asylum nestles in the sand. The celebration is there, the minister preaching, the new building for the women finished. People sit on folding chairs as he speaks, or lean against cars, or rest on the tailgates of trucks. The man who has killed at least fifteen stands and says this is the first place he has been treated as a human being. The man who lost his fingers to gangrene and his soul to heroin stands and says this place saved his life because when he came here he was dead.

Elvira, the cook, is short and fat and dark and poor and today wears a black apron and red t-shirt and blue sweat pants and she says when she stays home on her day off she feels so alone.

Out back run the coops made of scrap wood, cast-off wire, blankets, busted mesquite limbs. Ducks and chickens and a tom turkey look out. In the shadows, a man sits with the birds on a small stool. Fifteen feet down, a tall, lean man stands. He speaks softly to the pigs for an hour or more.

The minister says he recycles people.

The lean man speaks softly to the pigs.

Crossing the Line

I park on the edge because they are here in the early morning light. The white machines with the green band dot the parking lot. I have been careful coming in. The creek bed is now infested with agents, six or seven will cruise by sometimes during my morning walk.

At the store, the parking lot is Border Patrol machines. They are buying water, pop and food for a day of sitting on the line.

I tell him to stay in the truck.

He nods.

He is very calm.

I get him pants and shirts and socks. A cellphone with an unlimited thirty-day card. Food. A can opener. A small black backpack.

I come back with food.

I begin to float. I leave the laws.

He has finished eating.

I can smell the fear rising off him.

* * *

I stand near the line. Queen's wreath blooms on the sunny patio all behind me. A sixteen-year-old took eight in the back here. He was in Mexico. The shooter, a US agent, was near where I now stand. They say the dead boy threw rocks and so killing him was necessary.

I climb up on the concrete footing, stare through the bars of the wall, sight down into Mexico, see that perfect shot. This is where the agent stood, the police have left green paint to mark the spot. On the Mexican side, people point out the bullet holes for me. A mural faces the murder scene with a skeleton wreathed in black clutching a scythe while a crouched figure blows a bugle.

A Mexican guy walks past.

I ask, "Is this the place?"

He says, "Yes."

* * *

The heat comes up in my face off the rock.

A jet scorches past a hundred feet off the ground where I crouch beneath the scant cover of a creosote bush. This is the place the military trains pilots to hit targets. When I crossed into their country, I pulled up ground sensors. Waves of heat blur the horizon.

I wait for the sound to ebb.

I look down and see footprints heading north.

* * *

She sank to the floor terrified of the knives she would face in surgery and tugged at my leg for what she thought might be the last time. The building was an old adobe, and she'd been so happy moving into it because the mud home fit into some dream she had long had, a place where life would get smooth and joyful.

When my old man sat at that kitchen table and rolled that cigarette after they chopped at his face and mouth and his quick speech was gone for good, then, there was nothing but life and the love of life.

He struck a match, inhaled.

He died in a hundred days.

* * *

I can't get him to leave.

He calls his aunt. He stalls. I've run him up from the line. He's got his new clothes, food, his new backpack, a hundred bucks I gave him.

We are down by the river, against the bosque. A mile or two north on the other side of the river is the checkpoint stuffed with agents, dogs and laws.

The cool of the morning lingers under the trees. I lean against my truck as he makes another call. Cars go by, the faces glance over, faces white and thin-lipped. The country club spreads just the other side of the river. I can read in their eyes: that's a wet.

I tell him it is time.

He ignores me.

Maybe he thinks God protects him. Maybe he's just tired of the fear, of being hunted. The bottomland here was once full of grizzlies. They killed them out. The river was strong and rich with beaver and malaria. They've all but bled it dry.

From here, he walks forty miles. Then hits a city, then he gets to Los Angeles. Or Atlanta.

We agreed if they take him down, he never met me. We agreed when riding here, if pulled over I know nothing about him.

We skip last names.

* * *

I am nervous leaning against the truck. They may come.

A fat man wearing a t-shirt comes off a dirt track on his ATV. He has a gray beard. He glares at me. And at the brown man on the phone.

I turn to the brown man and say, "Vaya con Dios."

He uses his only English words, "God bless you."

And disappears into the trees.

Cortes

She translates, “Is this all?”

The surviving nobles have come. The city is gone, the Spaniards have destroyed it block by block. During an earlier stay, they had gathered much gold. Then, they had to flee and much of this gold was lost in the waters as they fell from the causeways in their panic. Now, the Spaniards are presented by the survivors with heaps of objects but it is not enough for Cortes and so he speaks and Malinche asks, “Is this all?” He orders that the Mexica return the gold lost during that bloody night of retreat.

There are a hundred thousand dead Mexica, or perhaps, two hundred thousand. The Spaniards may have lost eighteen hundred men in the long war to conquer Mexico.

A feast is in order. There will be wine from Spain, also pork. There will be maize and turkey. The feeding will be in Coyoacan on the mainland.

The men drink heavily, some walk on tables. Others fall down.

When the city falls, people flee and Spaniards roughly search them for hidden treasure—peering into nostrils for gold dust. But little is found. Rumors spread. Cuauhtémoc is tortured but says nothing.

Cortes thinks he will leave the city empty as a cursed spot.

But then he worries the ruins will remind the Mexica of what they once were. So he rebuilds.

Malinche marries a Spaniard and dies not that long after the conquest or Malinche marries a Spaniard and lives to be an old lady. Malinche becomes the byword for traitor, Cortes becomes the byword for monster.

My god the sky is blue.

On the concrete footing holding up the new wall thirty-one candles have guttered out at the place where a man stood and fired and a younger man on the other side of the fence took eight bullets in the back and died. Xerox portraits of other young men killed along the line rest beneath the candles. They all were said to have thrown rocks and for that reason the agents shot them dead.

The small row of candles and portraits is hard to notice.

The sound of sandhill cranes fills the air, the bugle call of the male, softer voice of the female and here and there the small call of the colt. Overhead long chains of cranes etch against the growing rose in the sky. Snow geese wait in the marsh, a great horned owl hides in a cottonwood with a mouse in its beak.

As sunrise nears, clouds of blackbirds, rusty and yellow-headed, swoop over the marsh.

The sun rises, group by group the cranes lift and head for the fields, the cold burns off, harriers begin to hunt the marsh.

Pyrrhuloxia feed in the thicket, deer move through the yellow grass.

Yellow-rumped warblers eat suet, a deer browses.

A heron stands by the edge of the pond dreaming of fish.

A man slides down the slope and comes out of the tall grass and I pretend he is not there.

A blue-throated hummingbird casts a shadow on my face at sunset.

The cranes are older than the rivers.

The cranes are older than the gods.

He asks me which way is Atlanta.

On Halloween in Ciudad Juárez, the people notice a man in black hanging from a fence. The next day they realize he is not a decoration but a corpse. The day after that other Mexicans gather in El Paso for the Day of the Dead. They put up that display in front of an old house, paper flowers, banners, an altar with photographs of their dead, a coffin covered with names. An old woman with a walker hobbles down the steps to the sidewalk and sits in a folding chair. Her face is stern.

The people gathered say, "This tragedy unites us, over there we have a history and over here we have nothing." Usually, an altar is made for someone who has died of natural causes or illnesses, but this is an altar for the assassinated, Mexicanos en Exilio would like to make known how many dead loved ones we have left behind. "This altar is but a mere representation because we do not have the option of leaving flowers on their tombs or waiting for our loved ones to come home. We have no home. This altar is a cry for justice."

The screen glows. A man stands and speaks. He is young, muscular, in his early thirties. He says he paid and they kept raising the price and finally he could no longer pay them.

So they came. They held him down and cut his feet off. He can't remember how, whether they used a saw or axe or machete. He simply can't remember that part.

His mother drove him north. He is in my country now seeking political asylum.

The money is gone and so are his feet.

The lawyer with the cancer continues to dab at his gums.

His mouth is dry from the radiation. He is weak from the chemotherapy.

He thinks the video will help raise money to protect people fleeing death.

The director leans over, says it is a first cut and he will trim some of the scenes.

The man watching dabs his gums.

The man on the screen is speaking in a calm voice.

The camera pans down.

He has no feet.

The woman tugs on my leg, her eyes full of yearning, the old man is dying without fear, his eyes full of curiosity and peace, the voice on the screen explains how he came to lose his feet, the Honduran vanishes into the bosque on his walk to a dream.

"God bless you," he says in his faltering English.

No one is going to be forgiven.

Masses will be said in Paris.

The Agents

He sits at the top of the U-shaped table and twenty-six people listen. The shirt is blue, the moustache trimmed, the face expects rapt attention. The meeting is in the government building by the bridge. The water runs high, brown with dirt, rich in chemicals. His official face hints at a smile as he explains the problems. Tons of beans must cross the bridge from the north, all donated to a charity and of course under the law there is no tax. But things must be worked out. It is not as simple as some might think and he is here to conduct the necessary business. The windowless room has no clock and time moves slowly as he speaks. A table against the wall holds water and a tray of cookies.

His cell phone rings, he looks briefly at the number, then holds it up over his head and continues speaking. The woman rises and comes swiftly to his side, plucks the phone and bends over to take the call. The air in the room is empty of life. As are the fluorescent tubes glowing overhead.

There is a priest who until very recently worked in a village just down the river. He said the hard part was saying a funeral mass when the coffin held nothing but a severed head.

People in the meeting listen with faces blank. The women are slow to smile. They are here to attend and be silent.

I walk along the creek thinking of shooting officials, look down and see an insect about to be crushed by my boot and carefully skirt it. Ants crawl over the snake flattened by traffic.

The official has the abundant flesh of a man who eats and eats often. I listen as he rolls on. He never doubts the importance of his words.

I sit in a diner at midnight during the early whispers of fall. The stars seem nearer now and colder and I hear sometimes voices from tombs on moonless nights. A man about sixty stares at the screen on the wall behind the counter. Someone has gone into a building and killed a bunch of people and then shot himself.

The guy says, "They're just running this to take our guns away."

I offer, "Tell that to the dead."

He scowls and turns away.

The meeting room is stale with the odor of soaps and disinfectants, of constant mopping to drive away the beasts and the dribbles and juices and the paw prints of what is out there, of our stench and scents and perfumes, of our hungers when naked and drool spills from our eager mouths. The room is a void, a place emptied out of life and smells, and there is nothing really in the air at the meeting. The windowless walls shelter us from the people screaming. In the room no one can smell the raw sewage snaking through the city.

The agents gather around their machines. To the south is the line. They will hunt into the night. But always I seem to do nothing and this drives my need to kill. I go to meetings and say nothing to the bosses.

All but two of the women in the meeting wear high heels, only two of the men wear suits.

Or there is this man with no legs. He holds a press conference. And says he is ready to ride. His new jeans mask his artificial legs. His smooth face belies his memory of the hacking at his limbs. An old woman comes down the stairs with her cane. She birthed ten children, six are now dead from bullets fired by the state.

There is a snap. I get out of my chair in the room overlooking the stream, walk over and see the crushed neck of a mouse in the trap. Dawn is still an hour away. Yesterday, along the creek I found a blue plaid blanket from Mexico near the spent rope from an earlier cache of drugs. The rope is aged by the sun. The blanket is new and from a recent visitor. I move off to where the herons roost and find a fresh encampment—tin cans, a worn out shoe, the remnants of a small fire, all the signs of the migrants moving north on foot.

Each day I can help people or beasts or I can do nothing.

What I can never do is ask if my efforts matter. That is forbidden.

Help is the right thing to do. To seek significance for one's acts is to kill hope and one's own life.

The state falters, the voices grow shrill or the voices choke and there is weeping. Help. Or do nothing and be nothing.

I no longer have a country.

I have ceased to be loyal to my species.

I know I have snapped.

It happened to me. There is no going back.

Not for me.

Not for them.

I belong to the place I was warned not to go.

I mix blood with the outlawed.

The air explodes as a military plane scrapes the sky and breaks the barrier of sound.

A great blue heron lifts off and slowly wings down the stream.

I am on native ground.

I finally stand up.

PART III
The Beauty Part

White butterflies hover over a patch of mud on the last crisp days of winter. They dance in a state of grace, sometimes rising up in the forest in a sudden column spinning over a pile of fresh dung. In the heart of the day when some warmth touches the soil, the mud wafts up as scent and intoxicates with the promise of seed and plant and flower and lust, all coming like a fresh shower on the day the lilies bloom. The white butterflies flit through an open door that was there in my earliest childhood and then slammed shut by some hand I do not know.

Beauty is not caged.

By now the cranes have gone through that hole in the sky.

I remember those last moments in the fields of corn, coyotes hiding in the wall of brown stalks, the cranes feeding where the crops had been knocked to the ground. Here and there languished wings and heaps of feathers from birds slaughtered while blinded by food. Dust flies, the birds claw the earth. An adult pair keeps watch over their smaller colt. Rattle calls thunder from the flock, the tumble of low notes that can reach out over two miles. When they are overhead, the call rakes the world and a big lonely seizes the heart. The cranes make us all strays and abandoned children as they glide into the blue.

In a bar, once a hunter told me he could not shoot a crane.

I did not ask why.

To see them is to know they are part of your life and that to shoot them is not murder, but suicide. This feeling for them is unexpected. They are tall, gawky and their voice a growl in the sky. They stare and never smile. But they are us and we know it at first sight and this fact invades our life.

Out there, in that field, the cranes eat and the beauty part lives just beyond my reach. I see but I do not smell or taste or hear the music of the sun. I am looking at a screen and I cannot seem to reach past into the thing itself. I am living by rote. The beauty part erupted inside me when the man mentioned the world behind the black metal door. I abandon my days and nights and go off looking for some new place. I will get to that.

He said that they eat their own shit.

And with that I was off.

Vincent van Gogh

Vincent van Gogh is part of a family that does not belong, the son of a Dutch Reform minister in a heavily Catholic village in southern Holland. He is home-schooled and wanders the heath of peasants living in dirt huts. He works in the family garden, a part of Dutch life, where each child is assigned his own patch and duties.

He goes on to paint garden after garden.

He never possesses one.

The child wanders a garden framed by a beech hedge and past that the flat world by the sea is fields of rye and wheat flowing. The boy lives on a plain and dreams of mountains.

In the parsonage garden, he sees marigolds, geraniums, golden rain. His mother favors yellow and red. And then come the raspberries, blackberries, and the apple, pear and plum trees. The rich soil, once sea bottom, explodes plants into flower.

Later, as a young man, he dreams of "a homeland . . . a small spot in the world where we are sent to stay."

Later, he will say, "I am a traveler going somewhere and to some destination . . . the somewhere and the destination do not exist."

Later still, he will cut off that lobe on his ear and wind up in an asylum. He will paint irises, blue flowers screaming out of the dirt.

He is dedicated to the color black and is appalled when the Impressionists insist black does not exist in nature and so cannot be part of the art that responds to the moment. But he is used to being the outsider. He says of himself, "He is a foul beast. All right—but the beast has a human history, and though only a dog, he has a human soul. . . ."

He has the hunger of those behind the black metal, those lying there in the cold eating their own shit.

He believes, "The journey of our life goes from the loving breast of our Mother on earth to the arms of our Father in heaven. . . . Has any one of us forgotten the golden hours of our early days at home, and since we left that home—for many of us have had to leave that home."

He repeats the book of Isaiah, "Can a woman forget her sucking child that she should not have compassion on the son of her womb?"

He aches for the beauty part but he cannot have it yet. He says, "I would like to leave some memento in the form of drawings and paintings. . . . *Something must be accomplished. . . .*"

First, he must fail and fail and fail. He must seem to others a madman. He must slice at his ear with a razor. He must go to the crazy place and stare out from behind the bars.

Then the iris will bloom.

The Beauty Part

The beauty part brushes against my life but stands off where I cannot seem to reach it. I plant seeds in the spring, haunt the dark woods, inhale the scents of woman and flower. I become crazed with dahlias and see bulbs as bombs to put in the soil. But the noise of my habits deafens me and I cannot hear the beauty. And I go on living my failure.

The pain of not creating beauty is great, more aching than loneliness. Birth and death come to everyone and they must experience both alone with no one that understands the sensation of those moments in those moments. But to never create beauty, to try and try and to fail. To fail at what a flower flings at the sky, to fail at what a bird sings at dawn.

There are small slivers that pierce my dull days.

The train track runs by the bar, the band plays outside as couples walk with buckets of iced long necks, the bottles brown, the ice white, the bucket galvanized. I want to brush my fingers against the metal. The women move on high heels, the big hair swaying. They have hungry eyes and trail perfume. The men do not smile. The honkytonk love flows, a freight train roars past. I walk out into tall grass, the music fades, trees loom black against the night sky. The stars overhead ache with beauty, the river murmurs below on limestone shelves. I want to jump and flow to the sea. Where the stream finally breaks free, the whooping cranes winter. They were almost extinct before anyone knew where they summered and bred when each spring they tore a hole in the sky and vanished north. Now they wobble on the edge of ruin.

The black trees against the stars bring me up short.

I remember my first murder—the cream-colored block over the blue bladder of the water bed with a dried drizzle of blood marking where the child's head hit the wall. A porn movie endlessly looped on the screen.

So I go.

The first blooms of the season struggle toward the light. I believe in snapdragons, pansies, wisteria plumes of lavender, early leaves on the grape vines, lilac petals sprinkling the ground. At dusk, the sun cracks the lake open and disappears without hiss into the dark waters. Rain comes off the plains, pelts the forests—fury of falling leaves—and drifts off seeking a desert to caress.

A whale breaches in the sea, the skin glistens, then rolls, dives, the waters close, and it's as if all this never happened. But still, it did.

There, just past my reach, there, the moment of beauty with harmony and grace. The water rises and licks against a red high heel while a macaw screams in the tree at the mouth of the garden. The river runs.

I look up.

A crane tears a hole in the sky.

The Garden

He leans on the table and tells of his dream. The wind is up, dust blurs the sierra. The cold hunts down everyone and blue smoke from the fires hangs over the city. The dogs huddle against the walls, the smoke from the kitchen licks the open ground behind the main yard. The men break from their work making paper-mâché apples and bananas and eat a plate of beans and tortillas. This is the safe place for the crazy people.

In the next room, a man tries to remember his past. We are waiting for him to finish. He is barred from entering the nation to the north but maybe the lawyers can find a hole in that wall. There is that stretch in Folsom, another one in San Quentin but what years? Deported twice but the dates are gone. Fifteen years in cells and he can hardly touch the memories. The murder in Georgia, that was dropped. Besides, he didn't do the killing. He was packing and had been drinking, that is true. But the dead guy went for his gun, and so the other guy shot him. But the details come hard. Life has been a careless series of days and nights. He has these letters somewhere, he'll find them because they have postmarks and dates and maybe then he can find his way back through the lost years before a river of alcohol and heroin washed around the hard ground of facts. It is not easy. He stumbled on an old girlfriend recently on a trip into the city. She looked at him with surprise and said she had thought he was dead.

In the yard, while the man goes through his interview, people drink the sun, their faces sometimes blank, sometimes full of mysterious happiness. The woman with no legs and one arm sits on the ground in the doorway and embroiders with her single hand, her smile red with lipstick. In the corner behind the black iron door are the people all but gone from this world. Their minds left long ago. And now their bodies slowly fail and they lie on the floor staring into eternity. The winter takes a heavy harvest. In part, the cold brings on the pneumonia. Also, the police bring those they find dying on the freezing streets to this shelter so they can be spared the paperwork of their deaths. One December ten people died in about a week. This is part of the season for the people of this place. They live just south of the border. The shelter with trucked-in water, limited heat and cooling is their best chance at a life. They eat three meals a day, sometimes medicine is available and no one kicks them or beats them or laughs at them. And they are touched by human hands. Sometimes one of the dogs that hangs around the shelter gets into the yard and people who never speak will touch the dog and begin to speak.

The man leaning against the table accepts all this, his dream is about a garden. The dream will not let go of him.

So here is the problem: design a garden for people who cannot speak, have been locked inside their own mind for years, sometimes decades.

The man says, "It is terrible. They just lie there in that room. Sometimes they eat their own shit."

He is working up to something. He is a believer and so the crazy people sprawled on the floor in the dying room are God's children moving off into eternity and he is sending them toward the tunnel of light and darkness called death without a pleasant image, a scent of the wild, a ray of sun on the skin, without the hint of love. They are behind the black metal door, on the cold floor without friends, without the touch of a fellow creature, a laugh, a sense of play. The minds sealed off and the dreams too private to be said.

He cannot know their desires. He lives an act of faith. The people behind the black metal door live the only life possible for them. They can do nothing for themselves. And what they can think is beyond the reach of others. He sees his world as a battle between Christ and Satan. The insane become seers in this world because they have crossed over from denial and sophistry. They live the madness others pretend is not happening. And so does he. His life has been mayhem. For years he created it with drugs, alcohol and violence. Now he seeks to stop the killing. But he has never been to the place where the people behind the black metal door live. He has caught traces of it, looked through the bars of a cell and tasted what a trapped life can be. But that is not enough to know the secret lives of people who have lost their minds and yet cling to life in the dark on that cold floor.

* * *

For years I have stared at images of the eagle nebula because it seems to rock me in the arms of eternity and because it seems to terrify me with the fires of hell. The spirals of gas and dust, the columns of fire in a star factory that astronomers call the Pillars of Creation. It is sighted by a Frenchman in the years before the American Revolution, in a time when the rivers of my country ran free and clear. Now our machines bring us closer to the thing as probes poke into its cauldrons and send us snapshots of worlds without end or beginning. That is where I always go for comfort, a boiling inferno framing a center swirling with color and eerie calm.

The wind blows. On the facing mountain a giant horse sketched with white disappears in the brown wall of dust. Everything is now cold, the chairs, the table on which the man leans, the floor, the walls, everything cold to the touch, the building has the feel of a corpse. Outside the sun a feeble disk in the sky, down in the pens the goats and hogs hide from this wind. Behind the black metal door in the corner of the yard where the crazy people wander, behind that it is even colder. They are dying without a word and nothing can be read in their eyes.

* * *

So he wants this garden, the one in his dreams, the place where they can leave this Earth and start on their journey to heaven. That is in his mind, heaven, the hell they are living in now, and the garden that they deserve.

Should it be the raked sand and stark boulders of a Zen meditation zone in a monastery? The lush flower beds of childhood? The city park on the first day school is out? The one in Eden with two trees, or Gethsemane where Christ paused before he met the cross?

Vincent van Gogh

In Belgium at Gheel, crazy people have gathered for centuries and melded into the town and by the time of Vincent van Gogh the town was called "The City of the Simple." When he went mad that first time, his father tried to ship him to Gheel. Then the place had 10,000 people, and a thousand of them were crazy.

There is a moment when Vincent van Gogh's father seeks to lock him up in the crazy place. The son is in his late twenties. He has not worked for five years.

He tells his brother Theo, "Well, that's how it is, can you tell what goes on within by looking at what happens without? There may be a great fire in your soul, but no one ever comes to warm himself by it, all that passers-by can see is a little smoke coming out of the chimney and they walk on."

Everything seems to be failure. He works for an art dealer but is let go. He teaches at a private school but they refuse to pay him. His family worries. He fits in nowhere. He decides to be a preacher. He is in London. He works for a minister who lets him give a sermon. Vincent van Gogh picks line nineteen from the 119th Psalm: "I am a stranger on this earth."

The Garden

I am in a stall in a border town. No one crosses now because the killing got bad. It is Saturday, the dust fills the empty streets. People either avoid my eyes. Or glare with warning. There is a small statue made of plaster, one maybe three feet high. The vendor demands $200 US and will not budge. The nation at that moment has over 500,000 people making motor vehicles for the rich people to the north. Each auto worker earns $16 US a day which means twelve and a half days on the line are required to buy the small statue of a man named Malverde who was hung far to the south in 1909. He is thought to protect those in the life who move drugs to the north, for the people who buy the automobiles also moved to the north. This hard kernel of fact means less than the dust in the wind. The blood is dry, the killing over for the moment, the slow death accepted as the drugs go north and so too the machines and statues are peddled to protect the soul in that dark wood we dread, the one we think lurks behind the black metal door, the one we deny lurks within ourselves. I move to escape the dark wood and it waits for me in the noonday sun. But I must not say this, others will shun my face. This must stay a secret, like the dreams flowering behind the black metal door.

Behind the black door, there on the cold floor with no sun lie the losers in this life, those who did not make the money or get the grades, those who may have had a love offered at birth but such moments ended long ago when the darkness came and they were found wanting, at first by others and then probably by themselves and then even the sense of failure vanished as the darkness became all and memory slipped to a place hard for them to reach.

The priest leans forward, night has come down on the line. He was run out of the country to the south because he stood for the poor against the man at a place called Bald Hill, a mesa near the line where global trade erupts out of the ground and buries the huts and lives of others. The rich man eventually put up a big fence with gun towers, there was some killing and then the priest was exiled north because he did not mind his manners. He had already been around. There was the time no one could understand a woman who washed up on the line and the priest reached her with fluent Mandarin from some stint in China.

So the priest leans forward, he is of a piece with the people waiting for death in the hard room behind the black metal door, couldn't name their own mother, the people of no account on that highway to heaven now and he is one of them, that is his work, being one of them, an outcast and there are these kind of priests out there, lost boys who thought Christ meant what he said and so left the building and joined him and his fellow outlaws on the Jerusalem road. There is that priest from Bolivia who spent close to forty years in the highlands and like the priest tossed from Mexico he has the same response to this new Latin American pope and his talk of the poor, that the church was waking up from a trance.

That is the reason for the garden for the people dying behind the black metal door at the asylum, the people who seem to like vegetables, the people finally going home to that beginning, that first sunrise when all the birds sang and shook the trees with joy, that garden, that time, that snap of the fingers and the trance ends.

Sometimes the waking up is a shock. He tried to kill himself come spring and then they put him in a hospital for crazy people named Green Stick and this place had a garden with nothing living in it, a glare of crushed rock and walls, and the place itself had the feeling of a bad waiting room. The faucets in the bathroom shower were recessed to slow down efforts at hanging. The air was stale, much staler than at the crazy place on the other side of the line where people lounged on the dirt in the winter sun, wood smoke floating across their faces and the one-armed woman did her embroidery. But in that place there is this flicker of garden dreams and in Green Stick there is nothing, nothing. Except electro-shock, explosions of energy in his head that were to save him from himself and from the darkness, session after session. Until the money ran out and then he was kicked out the door because a lot of being sane is not having the money to pay for being crazy. At least it is that way north of the line. South of the wall being crazy gets you nothing as a rule but then for most people being sane gets nothing, the poverty is fairly distributed among the crazy and the not crazy.

The Song of Solomon

Years ago, an old woman in a poor village gave me a print of heaven and hell because she said I needed the lesson. Her windows had no glass and desert heat burned fire in the air of summer. She was on the road to heaven, she was sure of that. In the drawing, the harlots, the drunkards, the card sharks, the rich, all staggered down the path to the burning lake where devils waited. They all looked happy. Another column draped in white robes wandered upward toward heaven. They all looked like Monday morning. The village itself was the standard model for drugs and money with fine horses, new trucks, and appliances run off car batteries. It was a place of horse-drawn plows and mansions rising from the dust of centuries. No strangers were invited and those who did stumble in were lucky if they got out alive.

At night, the stars sang and the old woman was certain the devil marauded and took the unwary. He was said to have hidden treasure in the nearby sierra and those who looked risked their souls and those who found the treasure never came back down to the village. God was very near there and so were memories of that first garden.

The little valley was overcrowded with killings, they were whispered among the people, the story repeated but always said ever so softly.

This was holy ground, a place of magic that had tortured the hopes of early missionaries and now flamed up in the day and the night in the sacred smoke of marijuana and the guns and bullets the smoke bought and paid for.

Solomon's song rang out:

> I am the rose of Sharon, and the lily of the valleys.
>
> As the lily among thorns, so is my love among the daughters.
>
> As the apple tree among the trees of the wood, so is my beloved among the sons. I sat down under his shadow with great delight, and his fruit was sweet to my taste.
>
> He brought me to the banqueting house, and his banner over me was love.
>
> Stay me with flagons, comfort me with apples: for I am sick of love.

There is a point where we must erase ourselves or never get to the hard ground of understanding. If life is about us, it is not about much at all but ecology and cosmology and any day crawling in the garden or walking in the silence of the winter woods. And if life is not about us, the exit from life, the path leading to the garden and away from the garden, the life beyond the cold floor behind the black metal door in the asylum, that design of succor brings us to a place past gender, past religion, past culture, past time itself, to a place as rich and mysterious as the womb that rocked us with dreams for months before the light of day blazed into our bleary eyes.

Vincent van Gogh

Her father is the king and when her mother dies he is very sad. He is of the old faith, his dead wife a Christian. They say his mind slips in his sorrow. He seeks a woman like his dead wife. This is not easy. Then he finds what he seeks. He wishes to make his daughter, Dymphna, his wife. She flees along with a priest, crosses the water and lands in Belgium, finds sanctuary in the town of Gheel. She builds a hospice for the sick. This lays down a trail of gold coin. When her father arrives, he has the priest killed and then cuts off his daughter's head. She is fifteen.

She becomes a saint. The town becomes a place for crazy people where they fit in with the sane. The town becomes the place Vincent van Gogh will not go.

He cannot find his destination, ever. This makes all our hearts gently weep, all of us who know he is right, that we are all heading somewhere and none of us, not a single one, can say with certainty where this destination will be found. Going, yes, going is always the mystery. The crane vanishing through a hole in the sky, the people on the floor behind the black metal door living in a place all their own, a place we can imagine but not know.

Van Gogh tries to dream a life of color—powder blue sheds, yellow stubble, pink skies—but the fears and dark things drag him down.

He thinks, "Why, I ask myself, should the shining dots of the sky not be as accessible as the black dots on the map of France? If we take the train to get to Tarascon or Rouen, we take death to reach a star. One thing undoubtedly true in this reasoning is this: that while we are *alive* we *cannot* get to a star, any more than when we are dead we can take the train."

The Garden

I want the garden I never crawled in, one with plantings richer than the tree of knowledge, a place beyond the spices and flagons and scents of Solomon's song. Like music and love, the garden must be past words, the garden must destroy words.

The garden must defy. If the garden reinforces our beliefs, if the garden pats us on the back, then the garden must be destroyed and pushed into the burning lake.

There is another time in a drug village, this one down by Sinaloa. The hills were pocked with the red blooms of poppies. The hamlet has new trucks, stereos, televisions, all run off car batteries again. And what strikes me is how little changes, how the poor become not different with the rush of money suddenly tumbling through their lives, but huge versions of their former selves. Around each adobe house was a garden protected by ocotillo wands, a barbed leafy barrier, and behind them bloomed the rose that Solomon knew, and blazes of bougainvillea. Chickens still pecked the ground but now the local horses were blooded and outfitted with fine saddles and silver stirrups. The small world had changed and not changed at all.

The man leans on the table and mentions the dying on the floor behind the black metal door, and I think how do you comfort people broken by the blows of life. And I think how do you comfort anyone with a garden? And I wonder if the purpose of the final garden is to comfort or to propel one on a path not yet taken?

The great landscape minds that gave us Central Park, or Versailles or the Boboli expanse in Florence, sought to free us from our terrors and stress and hard rubs with life. The final garden, like that first crawl into the desert of our life, should hurl us toward the thing life has never delivered but always promised.

The cranes are leaving. Each day I feel them departing. The sun rises sooner, the trees are in bud, and the cranes are leaving. Their calls are vanishing from the sky, they are streaming up from Chihuahua, moving over the place of the crazy people, the guttural sounds possibly penetrating the black metal door and reaching those drifting toward death on the cold floor, the cranes have been coming and going for millions of years, they have seen many gardens and yet still yearn for some place they have yet to reach. Aldo Leopold in those final days before he collapsed fighting a prairie fire on his salvaged Wisconsin farm got the cranes right by realizing he would never get them at all: "Our ability to perceive quality in nature begins, as in art, with the pretty. It expands through successive stages of the beautiful to values not yet captured by language. The quality of cranes lies, I think, in this higher gamut, as yet beyond the reach of words. This much, though, can be said: our appreciation of the crane grows with the slow unraveling of earthly history. His tribe, we know now, stems out of the remote Eocene. The other members of the fauna in which he originated are long since entombed within the hills. When we hear his call we hear no mere bird. He is the symbol of our untamable past, of that incredible sweep of millennia which underlies and conditions the daily affairs of birds and men."

Vincent van Gogh

There is a time before he goes crazy or maybe it is simply a time before others think Vincent van Gogh is crazy. He is in his twenties, living in Isleworth just outside of London, and working at a school for boys. He sees the soft light of morning, the garden threaded with gossamer, the sun flashing on the roofs and windows. He has failed working at an art dealer. He thinks he will become a preacher.

He's on the eve of his first sermon, one he plans to base on John Bunyan's *A Pilgrim's Progress*, or more precisely on a painting he has seen that captures the book.

He will open his mouth and preach that, "It's getting on towards evening. A sandy road leads over the hills to a mountain on which one sees the holy city lit by the sun setting red behind the grey clouds of evening."

He will say that a pilgrim on that road seeks the city, the man is weary. On the road a pilgrim who wants to go to that city, he is already tired, and "He is already tired and asks a woman in black, who is standing by the path and whose name is 'sorrowful, yet always rejoicing,'

'Does the road go uphill then all the way?'

'Yes to the very end'

'And will the journey take all day long?'

'From morn till night my friend.'

"The landscape through which the path runs is very beautiful, brown heathland with birches and pine trees here and there and patches of yellow sand, and in the distance mountains against the sun."

Van Gogh reaches. He can sense the room behind the black metal door and this frightens him.

But he seems able to reach past that room.

Vincent van Gogh is in love with this woman of the streets. He is the son of a minister and his family cannot abide this choice of his, but still he will not let go, no, he keeps love in an iron grip.

"Oh," he writes his brother Theo, "I am no friend of present-day Christianity, though its founder was sublime—I have seen through present-day Christianity only too well. That icy coldness mesmerized even me, in my youth—but I have taken my revenge since then. How? By worshipping the love which they, the theologians, call sin, by respecting a whore, etc., and not too many would be respectable, pious ladies. To some, woman is heresy and diabolical. To me she is the opposite."

There is a place where the beauty part lives and in that place there is sin and they eat shit and the birds always sing, even after midnight when the moon goes black.

The Garden

I have lived in a trance with the woes of the world. I have lived in a trance with my laziness and fear of learning. I have lived in a trance as drugs made my eyelids heavy.

Now, comes morning, the trance must end, the eyes look past my world into the worlds buried in the stone tombs and seething with new dreams in the fire and gases exploding beyond the vault of heaven. Beethoven, stone deaf by 1825, faced the nature of such a garden in his Grosse Fugue, a piece disdained at its premiere by an audience Beethoven called "Cattle! Asses!" Not that he watched them—he spent the premiere at a nearby bar drinking.

It took a century for the composition to find its audience, people conditioned by two world wars, death camps and gulags to believe chaos flowed through the very veins of the world. The piece, jagged and full of clangor, also is shot through with hope. Beethoven stands on a distant shore where the exhilaration of the revolutions meets the cold steel and murder of Napoleon. He is the man who sings while slogging through a land of gore and greed and hereditary fools.

In the last garden, the Grosse Fugue will sound like the songs of humpback whales that use the sea floor to bounce across the oceans of the Earth, the dissonance will be honey to the ear, the thunder the whisper of hope, and cranes will slowly beat their huge wings overhead, the deep calls punch through the millions of years and bring the fossils of the rock to the flesh of the moment, the peace of the garden was never in Eden—the folks left and there is the cold case where Cain slew Abel—and it is not in the cities or the wilderness areas or the whiskey bars with neon glow and perfumed women, the peace of the garden is touched by the Grosse Fugue, a buzz saw cutting a groove through time to some core where we have to make landfall, and the opening notes make a flying leap into this unknown, a move keeping pace with cranes arcing across the blue to other worlds, and coming back from the entrails of our world. In 1900, a monk works on frescos in the Cave of the Thousand Buddhas and finds a secret chamber rich with ancient manuscripts and from this dust and stale air "The Crane Maiden" flies back into the minds of people. A man helps a wounded crane and then later comes the knock at the door, the beautiful maiden, love and marriage and the maiden makes wonderful tapestries, but no, no, the husband is forbidden to ever watch her weave but, here the tale varies ... the woman craves her wild life and abandons husband and child for the skies ... the husband peeks and discovers his wife is a crane plucking her own feathers to make the tapestries and when she finds him watching she flies away into the heavens where only cranes can go. There is a species of crane that crosses 47 countries in its annual migration and still we cannot get close to its world no matter how many maps we make.

The Bible can only envy the world behind its claims of the spirit.

Isaiah 38:14 says, "Like a Crane or a swallow, so did I chatter: I did mourn as a dove ...."

Jeremiah 8:7 says, "The stork in the heaven knoweth her appointed time; and the turtle and the crane and the swallow observe the time of their coming."

And now the time comes, the time to leave the cold floor behind the black metal door and burst out into the light and fury, to find that deep wingbeat that has coursed over the face of eons, the voice beckoning, a sound Aldo Leopold thought the trumpet in the orchestra of the wild and the free, and yes, the garden, the last garden must upend what has been and become what we cannot imagine, the dissonance now a harmony, the clangor now soothing to my new ears.

The purpose of the garden is not to aid leaving one life for another or to ease a life into a death, the thing has to be about wonder, that first sensation when time began also must be the next sensation. A life should have more wonder than fear. Rolling and tumbling, dogs and people, clouds of butterflies, gases exploding into arcs of energy called nebulae, that is the garden, not serenity, not terror but hunger, that glowing hunger at the first light of the life, the hunger that can never be satisfied and for which there is no menu, the garden that flows not out of us but into us, the garden waits beyond our plans, it is in the dreams behind the black metal door when the crazy people sleep on cold floors, it is in our eager eyes that first morning of our time on earth as we wail with hunger and plot the sudden revelation of desires.

The rains do not come much anymore. The ground cracks, the ruins sleep, the constant cracking in the dark, and in the night the trees also cry and writhe. This will never end, just as it never began. But once in a great while in the desert around the asylum, the rains fall from heaven and then hell booms out of the earth beyond the room with the black metal door.

The facts are brittle things and I cling to them in hope and yet they snap in my hand and litter the ground. Bodies have belched out of the desert around the crazy place in the past few years. They have flesh and then at times they are simply bones. They had mothers and fathers but now they have no names. In the darkness, coyotes howl over the meat and the dogs of the asylum venture out to find them for the choicest parts of the corpses. And in the center of the caterwauling, the water smooth as glass, Canadian geese float there, yes, back there where the trees stand in water and the bony branches shake down some shade against the sun. Pintails dive, as do buffleheads. Canvasbacks drift in small squads, mallards lounge on the banks and overhead hawks search the living for the one soon to be dead. The sky drips blue. The cranes are gone, they funneled up into a hole in the sky and now have vanished into another world. The cormorants return, they dry their wings on old stumps above the green water. On the broken stalks of the spent fields the carcasses of cranes form gray mounds of litter. Soon the wind will take the remains and all will be smooth again like the water in the ponds. The turtles emerge and bask, warblers flit with whispers of spring beating out from their wings.

I try to grab hold but this is not possible because all around the calm the coyotes scream as the dead come out of the ground and night falls, the dogs are out there fighting for their share of the flesh.

I sit outside on an old car seat in the sun, the wind whips, dust swallows mountains and one dog comes over, the coat a rich rust and thick, he is the leader. Once he brought in an arm, the muscles still attached, the meat red. Another time it was a head. In all he has fetched six of the dead back from the night and the coyotes. When the blackness falls, people out on the campo think they see police cars come and go and this may be the source of the bodies.

He says the people in the room behind the black door spend years in there, naked, on the floor seeing nothing. He can't stand this, they must see the sky from a garden.

We are in a café. He has plans now for the garden, a winding walk, trees, there will be a fountain and speakers playing soothing music. He has men making blocks behind the asylum. The wall will be three feet high and there will be metal columns that are higher spaced along this wall. He drives fast, the fever is on him, the desire to get something done. The garden will face north, toward the whitewashed horse on the mountain and toward the highway so the people will hear trucks and cars and the noise of the living.

He has plans for a path that will lead from the room with the black metal door to the garden. The people will be carried out each day and some will lie in the sun, some in the shadow, the sound of water, the sound of big trucks, the sound of the wind, that soothing music, also. They will feel the sun after years in darkness.

He plays a sample of the music that will comfort the dying. Then he produces the song that keeps him going. In this song a man remembers when he was young and remembers his young love and how things did not work out as he hoped but he keeps going "I began to find myself searchin'/searchin' for shelter again and again" and now he has his shelter in the asylum, the cure for the emptiness that once stalked him and he is surrounded by people that also found that fabled thing, community, and they are misfits, some crazy, some killers, some addicts but now all are whole in this place in the desert south of the line and beyond the eye of the workaday world.

The geese float on the clear water under a blue sky. There is no sound louder than the flapping of wings as ducks lift and move across the pond. Hawks watch, the cormorants are back, the cranes vanished into a hole in the sky. The wind is down.

In the garden, he plans long benches and the people from behind the black metal door will lie on these benches and search the sky. He does not know what they will see. Or think. One of his helpers argues the whole idea is pointless, that the people behind the black metal door know nothing and see nothing and think nothing, that they are like vegetables pulled from the garden behind the asylum.

The man sits and listens to Bob Seger sing "Against the Wind." He cannot accept that the people know nothing and feel nothing even though he knows his helper may be right. But still, he has to think something reaches them, and that given how little they get from this life, a garden, the roar of trucks, the sun and shadow, the sound of water, some music, could mean everything to those we find to be nothing.

I am back.

Where I began.

The corpses belching out of the ground when the rare rain comes, the coyotes scream, the dogs fight for the flesh and in the center, the calm eye of the water, smooth with faint ripples left by geese and ducks, the blue sky bouncing back off the surface.

The last garden, soft music, tumble of water.

Air brakes roaring on the trucks hauling freight into the hours of night.

He leans on the table and tells of this dream.

Vincent van Gogh

He looks up and feels dread. He looks up and feels hope. Van Gogh goes back and forth on what he finds in the night sky. He is in Arles, the place of light in the south of France, the place he will lose his earlobe and then his mind and then his life.

He looks up.

He thinks, "I have the thing in my head, a starry night; the figure of Christ in blue, all the strongest blues, and the angel blended citron-yellow." But he can't pull it off. He tells himself it is too beautiful to paint, then, he paints the scene and fails and scrapes the paint off.

But the stars come back. Paris had no night sky. But in Arles, he finds night brings black—"the town disappears and everything is black"—and then come the stars storming in his mind.

He writes his sister he wants to create a place "under the great starlit vault of heaven" where there can be work, love, sex. He puts in Ursa Major. He paints also the Big Dipper. He solves the problem of the starry starry night simply.

He removes Christ from the painting. And fits in the shadowy form of two lovers on a black shore.

A Hole in the Sky

Vanish through a hole in the sky. The cranes fly above history and follow a road in the sky. They began their migration before the river was made. The people behind the black metal door vanish through a hole in their minds and they follow a road for which we have no maps.

The cranes can visit the heavens, the earth and the underworld. They can fly at 20,000 feet. They migrate thousands of miles. They vanish through that hole in the sky.

They come from Mexico, the Gulf Coast, the deserts and with slow wing beats, low rumbles of calls, course over the plains, a sweep of grassland and pivot irrigation with cathedral towns huddled around giant granaries, the God of this place. The birds are all but gone, the grasslands uprooted for wheat and corn, the rivers murdered for the fields and towns. The original people have largely vanished, the buffalo are kept in little memorial patches. A meadowlark sings into the wind above the jagged ridge of the Smoky Hill River. The Pawnee, Sioux and Comanche hunted here. When gold was found in Colorado, the Smoky Hill became the corridor as men rushed to bonanza dreams.

The cranes fly over, fly south in the fall, fly north in the spring. They see mammoths go down to Clovis points, watch the cheetah make its last run after antelope, see Coronado wander onto the plains, see the Sioux and other buffalo nations rise up on horses and fresh robes, hear the dreams of the Pawnee, feel the wound of the Oregon Trail. By the end of the nineteenth century, they recede, cease nesting in the plains as hunters slaughter them for meat.

The cranes fly over El Quartelejo, the pueblo probably created by Taos and Picuris people fleeing Spanish rule in New Mexico in 1696. For ten years they stay safe from Spanish eyes and then the men come on horseback, round them up and march back to New Mexico. The cranes see it all. And they never come in.

They come down on the Platte in groups of fifty or one hundred or five hundred, low cries falling from the sky as they chase down the day at sunset, the river a copper ribbon, cold seeping into the bone, the bald eagle moving upstream with that last hope of a fish in its eyes, forty-two miles of roosts left out of three hundred, the river vanished long ago down the maw of cities and farms, the cranes, they fly over, they see everything, look past sundown into the deep time people scorn, the slow reverberation of life as it comes and goes, the beasts falling into oblivion and still the cranes fly overhead, the river goes red then orange pink slate gray and black, still they come, Canadian geese honk over the river, the cranes keep coming, the last great pulse on the plains, the tribes locked up, the buffalo murdered, the grasslands fields, slow wing beat overhead, three whitetail deer bound across the brown meadow in the dying light.

The modern human pathways across the plains run east and west, the various trails of pioneers and truckers. The routes of the buffalo cultures are slowly erased by the slashes of roads and fields. But the cranes keep to their highway in the sky.

I drive my life through the grass, slate-gray skies, old cafés with chipped mugs, pie cases needing cleaning, the freezing wind at the gas pumps, the sad main streets hurtling toward the sundown of their existence, old signs flapping, the barns lean with ads for chews no longer craved. Cattle huddle in the draws, the rivers flat and wide, the sky huge but then it lowers and storms spit tornadoes, or the sky goes blue, the rains stay away and the ground burns.

Always there is the sense history stopped long ago when the Indians fell, the pioneers crossed the prairie and moved into that little house, and then, then it was one day after another and church on Sunday, now and then a mad dog killer but no songs, the songs stop and the days just thud by, then the years stagger along and the farms get bigger, the towns shrink but everything seems to move to a museum because history ceased happening and the present became the yawning grave of time, cranes overhead, slow wing beat, their history unending, millions of years pile up, rivers come and go, the weather tilts this way and that way, they rise up, migrate, dance without end.

The last garden offers a chance for the beauty part but only for old beauty, known beauty, not for what the people behind the black metal door see, not for the dreams of cranes flying on the highway through the sky. There is a place out there with a music not yet heard, there is a place out there with a garden never imagined, there is a place out there I will never reach but always, always go toward.

The mystery is what I need, the sense of something beyond logic and maps, the world I imagine behind the black metal door and above as the cranes call out. When the time is right, they will ride a thermal up, test the winds, and if all is favorable they will vanish through a hole in the sky. And I cannot follow no matter what aircraft I commandeer because I cannot get to where they are going with a machine. The Platte dribbles along, a shadow of the river that once crossed the plains and was the artery for the Oregon Trail. Francis Parkman camped here, met the Sioux, rode his horse bareback and dreamed his big project, books that would capture the struggle between the French and the British for the wilderness empire of trees and prairie. As a boy, he fought frail health with four years in the forests of his grandfather's wilderness estate. He never escaped the bewitching memories of being a boy in the woods. He went home from his visit to the plains, set pen to paper and became a ruin who often could not walk or see. He battled headaches and insomnia and could not bear the slightest light. He worked in the dark, often dictating the wild ground from a blacked-out room. He raised roses, became an authority on Japanese plants, rowed in his pond when he could stand the light and made friends with a muskrat. And vanished into the forests of his imagination.

There is a time when I tend a dying dog who is incontinent, paralyzed and embarrassed by his state and for weeks I sleep on the floor with him and read the entire history of the war for the forests by Francis Parkman, a mix of beast and shit and men and trees wavering in the light of an open sky of blue, and I can still inhale his scent and still remember the blue covers on the set of Parkman's histories, the cranes fly overhead, I cannot follow but I can sense and out here in the cold—it is the first days of spring and a snow has fallen overnight—two robins worry a patch of grass under the light of a parking lot, cranes call overhead, skim ice coats the slow pockets of the river. The houses and towns here turn inward away from the breath of winter and the wind. This a world of brown and gray now, green will come on in a few weeks, then the surge of wheat and corn and sorghum, the ducks and geese flying Vs overhead in fall, and then the crust of winter driving everything inward again, a sense of pale lives, rooms without color, long nights of cold winds and then the cranes gather again, come from places far south and the river rattles with life, the dances begin, the courting accelerates.

And then they vanish into a hole in the sky.

Vincent van Gogh

He's almost to the dying part. He's about done with the beauty part, those crows winging over the wheat field will be his last painting. He has about figured it out and so he writes his brother Theo who is on the verge of his final dive into syphilitic insanity. Vincent thinks, "I feel more and more that we must not judge God from this world, it's just a study that did not come off. What can you do with a study that has gone wrong?—if you are fond of the artist, you do not find much to criticize—you hold your tongue. . . . This world was evidently slapped together in a hurry on one of his bad days, when the artist didn't know what he was doing or didn't have his wits about him. . . . And for this life of ours, so much criticized, and for good and even exalted reasons, we must not take it for anything but what it is, and go on hoping that in some other life we'll see something better than this."

I can sense everyone behind the black metal door—they even eat their own shit—suddenly listening.

The bones glow, a table full of skulls drinking in afternoon light from a west window. The javelina no longer mill with the herd, the deer have lost their big eyes looking for danger in the dusk. Birds take rest on the table, their flying days over. The graveyard has a beauty to it, the bones sculpture better than the stuff gathering dust in the art museums.

He is full of life as he shows off the bones. He came here looking for something and he found it. The air is clean and blue, the mountains near but empty. The lion still hunts the slopes, the eagle kills out on the grasslands. Come fall, the elk bugle and there is hope for the wolf to take back the country.

Everything pulses. The river just to the east is a corridor of cranes as they come and go through the holes in the sky.

The nearby saloon has a game of eight ball going. One ball rockets off the table and a player dives on the floor in a serene stab at a catch. He misses and crawls to the ball.

The barkeep says enough and throws him out.

The other players, all Indians, resume the game. The reservation is off across the plains just to the north.

The bone man has a scotch. This is his place, the sky outside, the grasslands, the mountains, the golden eagles sweeping down.

They take his phone calls for him here.

He's come a long way to find a place he can stay.

The wind is up outside.

All the cranes are coming back from the north country. Soon thousands will arrive. The ancient days begin anew with the sunrises and sunsets as the cranes move their ritual onto the winter ground.

He smiles.

I wonder if I can ever write anything as pretty as the bones on the table. He's put some kind of varnish on them and they glow like soft sun on a lazy afternoon. His face comes alive as he handles the bones on the corner table with the afternoon light lapping against their lives.

The hole in the sky hangs over all of us in the whiskey bar.

He thinks of what it is like to be a caged bird. He struggles to explain to his brother and himself why in 1879 or 1880 he shed his claims to normal careers and decided to be an artist. That time when his father wanted to commit him to an asylum.

Life feels barely begun and yet too strange to ever be within reach. There is music in the air but no one else seems to hear it. These sounds become colors but it is dangerous to mention this. Simple sentences seem like frauds as impressions—that scent, the soft pad of the cat, the green roaring off a head of lettuce, the crow murdering silence—jumble together into a truth stronger than logic or grammar. Love, hate, lust, these are sensed, they hang in the air everyone seems to be breathing, but no one else admits their presence. The dog in the barnyard understands and speaks but all the others are deaf to these clearly stated pronouncements. There are whispers all around, eyes stare, it is all so obvious. Behavior is watched and judged, deviants can be sent to the crazy place. Be careful, oh, so careful, don't even blink, arouse no suspicion.

Alone. More alone than a crane vanishing through that hole in the sky. More alone than the people on the cold floor behind the black metal door. Standing in the schoolyard, the new kid on the block. Facing a storm on the plains, the highway emptied and slowly the lowering sky obliterates the horizon. The day the firing notice comes down and everyone turns their backs and suddenly no one sees the person they had coffee with every morning for years. This feeling of not belonging, of not being wanted, of being strange and filed away as the other kind.

He rejects what they say of him. Vincent van Gogh senses he is strange but keeps this strangeness close to his heart. He writes his brother, "Life itself, too, is forever turning an infinitely vacant, disheartening, dispiriting blank side towards man on which nothing appears, any more than it does on a blank canvas. But no matter how vacant and vain, how dead life may appear to be, the man of faith, of energy, of warmth, who knows something and stays with it, will not be put off so easily. He wades in and does something and stays with it, he violates, 'defiles'—they say."

But the whispering continues.

Vincent van Gogh tells his brother Theo about what he knows that caged bird must feel. But then the season of the great migration arrives: an attack of melancholy. He has everything he needs, say the children who tend him in his cage—but he looks out, at the heavy thundery sky and in his heart of hearts he rebels against his fate. "I am caged, I am caged and you say I need nothing, you idiots! I have everything I need, indeed! Oh, please give me the freedom to be a bird like other birds."

Faure took a dance, made a song and now I listen from the upper seats as the orchestra plays "Pavane." As a child I couldn't understand how composers picked the notes. I thought they were simply flung down to fill space, like a bunch of grapes ripped off a vine. I was certain I could take fistfuls of notes from a score, throw them away and no one would notice or care. I still think that sometimes. But when the sounds get good I forget the composer because I am convinced the notes picked the person simply as a clerk to write them down. Words fail when music succeeds. There is much to hear and feel and think about but almost nothing to say.

The notes rain down from heaven even if God is dead.

Snow geese huddle in the tall grass, a white pelican paddles by, sea gulls arc over the strand of water, the notes keep clanging in my head, a stream of bangs, twangs, and peals, the colors swirl, I stand and go dizzy and reel with these new notes pouring out of the ground or is it from the sky, are the geese playing a piano? Do they notice music?

Beer cans under a rolling bolt of blue.

The big wind comes off the desert, the dust walls the sky, the doves go silent and huddle inside the trees. After midnight, the roar falls away and then suddenly a white winged dove tolls in the new still of the night. Van Gogh thinks "anything complete and perfect renders infinity tangible, and the enjoyment of any beautiful thing is like coitus, a moment of infinity."

A vermillion flycatcher alights on the barbed-wire fence. The river struggles, a wounded thing dying within its banks. Ducks flee me and overhead a call rattles the sky as seventy sandhill cranes in a V move north toward the breeding grounds. South, across a line, they lie behind the black metal door and outside the wall the garden slowly comes into being, dirt where they will feel sun and see sky before they become dirt once again.

Every time I seek the garden, every time I reach for the beauty part, things shatter. Suddenly I find pieces on the floor. I stare down at the shards cutting my feet, blood runs and I am baffled but not surprised. For a while, I thought others stopped me from writing the beauty part. Then I realized the only thing stopping me was me.

I was blind as I looked for the beauty part, I stumbled and fell. Then, here are moments when I feel things near, my breath grows short, my heart pounds and a fragrance brings me to my knees.

But the garden, that is a separate matter.

Van Gogh says, "I've done a garden without flowers, or rather a stretch of grass, just mown, very green with gray hay spread out in long rows, a weeping ash and some cedars and cypresses, the cedars yellowish and spherical, the cypresses tall, blue-green, and at the back, laurier rose and a corner of a blue-green sky. The blue shadows of the shrubs on the grass."

The garden the man plans for the people behind that black metal door—music, sun, sound of water—prepares them for the next place. That is the certainty of the man leaning on the table haunted by his dream.

Van Gogh paints many gardens. There is one just across the way where he knows the wayward girls meet their customers. When he touches the life coming out of the ground his words melt the ice in my heart because he reached the beauty part: "There are moments in between whiles when Nature is superb, autumn effects glorious in color, green skies contrasting with foliage in yellows, oranges, greens, earth in all the violets, burnt up grass amongst which however the rains have given a last energy to certain plants, which start again to put forth little flowers of violet, rose, blue yellow. Things one is quite sad not to be able to reproduce."

His last words are "the sadness will last forever."

The Killing Ground

The salt in the air, the ocean sounds soft laps of waves against the arc of the sandy beach. No one comes to the resort, this is not the season in Puerto Penasco. The bullet tore through Jesus while they hunted the dark man. The sea is calm now, the winds down, the sun morning warm. The fat cop stares and gulls wheel over the Gulf. Inside the door of the cream-colored villa, there seems to be blood on the bedroom rug, over there, just past the toys near the Christmas tree. Out on the sea in these waters, blue whales come, and at the head of the gulf vaquitas linger, a small tribe of porpoises with only a few hundred left on Earth. The volcanic range flows just to the north of the bullet-torn Jesus and the bloody rug. There are days there when the sun kills the soul and there are nights when the stars ring out like bells over the black desert.

The killings and the villa and the big towers of apartments stand like fangs against the sea and the desert and the life of the sea. The gunfire began before dawn, then the choppers hovered, then cars fled, men died, trucks burned. The sun rose and slowly crept across the sky.

Holes stare from the trunk of the sapling by the door. The facing wall shows the marks where a .50 caliber danced and shattered the concrete block underneath the stucco. The double front door, half glass, half wood, is battered and to the right a barrage frames the door to the bedroom. A big table in the living room is upended right next to the dried-out Christmas tree. There is a small wagon full of stuffed toys—some elves with Christmas caps, candy canes smiling with white and red stripes. Plastic party hats are scattered outside in the entryway.

I drive hundreds of miles to come here and I know I must and yet I do not know why I come. The sea, the crack of gunfire, bodies, blood, sand, and a hole in the sky. I sense these things but cannot say what holds them together. But in my mind they are and I come alive with this sensation. For the first time in weeks, maybe months I feel alive as I touch the links between things that I cannot say, even to myself.

Police tape blocks entry. That final night is shattered shortly before five a.m. a week before Christmas and the shooting continues for four hours. Or maybe longer. Helicopters hover and fire. Men on the ground fire. Dead bodies litter the road from the resort back into town, as do burned vehicles.

The killing is far away, and very near. The toys on the floor, the bullet holes, the baby Jesus shot as Mary and Joseph look on the abandoned nativity scene. A breeze comes off the sea, whales are plowing silently through the water and yet none of this is within reach, but simply must be imagined. Screams, shouts, choppers chuffing in the sky, crack of bullets, and then walk a hundred feet and nothing ever happened here but the silence of a resort in the off-season with an empty pool and lonely bar stools.

The killing ground is here and there and soon to be closer and closer and closer.

In Agua Prieta men come in machines and they fight in the night leaving wrecked trucks, blood, spent cartridges. Then news accounts flutter briefly. Then nothing more is said.

It is midday Saturday, the shops for tourists are largely closed, the sidewalks empty of people. A black truck with federal police rolls past, the men masked, in dark clothing and cradling automatic weapons. In the plaza, a few vendors peddle tacos.

Eyes follow the stranger.

Where did the shooting happen?

I don't know anything about that the voice says.

The air feels crisp but heavy.

There are no loud sounds.

There are hardly any sounds at all.

The sea stills after the storm but the beasts lurk in the deep and could explode to the surface without warning. The great calm masks the dread. And life looks normal but somehow off.

Out there the jellyfish are bobbing, brainless, without hearts or lungs, bobbing in the calm waters. They never change and now they are coming and taking the oceans. We have taken the things that eat them from the seas and now the jellyfish destroy the waters. There are now said to be over five hundred spots, marks on the oceans where jellyfish have forged a world that is death for others. The toxic blooms will grow. I am tumbling, over the edge, the speed increasing, a swirl of violence and want that soon reveals itself to be a new structure. The helicopters hover and fire at the villa darting back and forth behind the tower of apartments. The streets are empty after the night of killings and the stares are cold. The future is behind the black metal door or past that out in the last garden, the one we visit before life moves on to another place.

He fails and fails and fails. The man who gave the world that starry night and the explosions of sunflowers, that man knows failure after failure.

He thinks, "I have always had coarse animal tastes. I neglect everything for the external beauty of things, which I cannot reproduce because I render it so ugly and coarse . . . albeit nature seems so perfect to me. At present my bony carcass is so full of energy that it makes straight for its objective.

The result is a degree of sincerity, perhaps original at times, about what I feel, but only if the subject lends itself to my crude and clumsy touch."

We fail and we go behind the black metal door and we go out into that garden and then, just maybe then, we vanish through the hole in the sky. To touch a blade of grass is to get close. To understand a blade of grass is to go beyond the wildest hopes.

The beauty begins when we leave Eden. That is when we escape harmony and grace for the jagged edges of wonder. Everything breaks, beer cans litter the ground by the great river. The man in the other room remembers everything except where he has been. He remembers being a coward, a liar, a thief, but the dates are hard for him to dredge up.

I never forget my past but I abandon it constantly.

And I leave nothing behind.

Names, faces, empty bottles, manuscripts, notes on the movement of spring migrants through the coyote willows down by the river, all these things become castoffs, along with my dreams and broken shoelaces.

In Japan, if you fold a thousand origami cranes, your wish will be granted.

He wants to see his daughters again, the drugs and the violence, those are past. He is a new man and he lives in the asylum and tends to those behind the black metal door and those who live outside that door. If he can only remember the dates, and the charges also.

The cranes vanish through a hole in the sky.

* * *

The psalm is no. 91, "Nor for the pestilence that walketh in darkness; nor for the destruction that wasteth at noonday."

I pause. I strain to hear cranes overhead but the sky remains silent. The feathers do not cover me, the ancient song rings hollow and yet somehow strikes a chord within me. It is not because life must have meaning or God must be above all or disease and destruction walk the land. No, something else. Life must be for both me and the crazy people and the cranes overhead, all of us arcing to the same place under the same sky in the huge empty of a universe without borders.

* * *

They will be carried out and laid on slabs, the sun will dance anew on their lives, the trucks roar down the highway and water gurgles in the fountain. The sky so blue will ache overhead. And they will say nothing. They will tell us nothing. They will be in the garden we create but they will dwell in a place we do not know and cannot find on our own.

They say Moses wrote the 91st Psalm during his years in the wilderness and after enduring that plague of fiery serpents. The children of Israel had been baked by heat, raked by disease and evil vapors came in the night under the glow of the moon. There were scorpions and the rains did not come. Bears, lions and leopards stalked their camps. The wolves howl in the night and the devil moves through this desert.

I have not bent my knee in a church since age twelve and do not regret this fact. My Bible reading comes in motels with lonely nights and bad highways. I think somewhere in these ancient songs I will hear a few notes of the melody that once was life before some great mangling tore the score.

The feathers will cover me.

The cranes vanish into a hole in the sky.

The Cranes

The cranes sometimes sleep in. They breakfast al fresco. I have never heard one utter a bitter word. A friend tells me of manhandling one species at a zoo. He lifts up a hand to show his scars. In the fields of the refuge we have created so that the cranes can survive as we shrink their world, feathers lie in piles where coyotes have ripped cranes apart. The blue sky reflects on the still waters of the pond as two bald eagles stare from a dead limb. A great egret walks black legs through the fresh spring shoots of green.

Up up up fly the cranes and I stay on the ground paralyzed by my own cages. The garden will comfort those broken in mind and body, that is the goal. But no one knows where the people behind the black metal door fly when left to the wings of their own bodies and souls. But we will build the garden they need out of the rich ground of our ignorance. I hear cranes calling overhead, vanishing into a hole in the sky. They do not matter, they are beasts, they have nothing to say we must heed or need to know.

Cold wind, gray sky, then the sun slips through a slit, the water of the Platte turns gold, then copper, a robin sings from a black limb, the bass notes roll out of the throats of cranes and rumble the cottonwoods almost budding green along the wet loins of the plains. Fried cod in the bar, the click of pool balls, green felt in the stale air. Night has come down, hundreds of thousands of cranes stand in cold water and guard their sleep as they wait for the soft splash of a predator moving with eager fangs toward their warm blood in the night. Stars hide behind the clouds, the moon rises in secret and after midnight snow flutters down to whiten the first days of spring.

The Beauty Part

I can see him driving now, the radio on Hank Williams, a Lucky Strike dangling from his lips and he peers through his glasses at the ribbon of highway wandering up and down the hills of Iowa. The windshield is split, but still has a modern edge because it does not lift up from the bottom. The clock on the dash died long ago. Toward dusk, all that can be seen is the glow of his cigarette. "I'm so lonesome I could die," summer pouring through the open windows. I cradle a bottle of root beer, the haze of smoke pouring over the front seat. He drives with one hand on the wheel, the other on the lap of his girlfriend. She has black hair, a smile and smells clean. Her jeans are very tight but high-waisted in the fashion of that moment. A couple of recent wars are over and there is this spell when the guns go silent and birdsong returns.

The world for a moment is scent, smoke, song and a blur of farmsteads streaming past the open windows. Small things get big. The way my cousin flips his lighter with one hand and brings it up effortlessly to his smoke. The fact that the clock on the dash of the car is dead but the radio lives.

The loneliness is when you are with people; that is the hardest. But this trip back then in the mists is not like that. It is the road and it is love, there is a heat flowing between them. He's back from a war, he's left the small town for the big city, he has a quick mind and he can effortlessly light a cigarette while driving.

She is Catholic, he has no faith and this is a wall in those times, a barrier more harsh than the black metal door. There are all kinds of rules and all of them, every single one, slams a door in your face. There are these religions no one can explain that decide without saying so who can love who. The driver, my cousin, he is a warning. My mother says he could have been the class valedictorian but chose to be the class clown. She makes clear this was a terrible decision. But what I notice is the word play, the smiles, quips, laughter, that he has a clean-smelling woman with tight jeans sitting beside him on the drive and she is in love with him. There are these stories about how when he came back to his little Iowa town from Korea he would not talk and after he'd moved on and gone to the big city his folks found a cigar box full of medals in his dresser. Then there is one story he let slip about walking down a road and a truck comes by with dead soldiers in back bouncing like cordwood.

And the VFW halls where I sit and drink beer with him when he is older and I was older but his war is ever young and near and not to be spoken of. He bowls a lot, he picks up money as a cabby, he stocks cigarette machines, he does this and that. One night in the cab, a guy pulls a gun. He quits after the shift. Money isn't worth a bullet. He laughs about it. Everything is a quip.

There is the night he almost bowls a three hundred game in the league and that is the only time I see him swell when he tells of the game and shows the score sheet he's snagged as a trophy. The medals in the cigar box seem not to mean much. The ball rolling down the lane, the pins exploding, that means a lot. He cracks a joke, one hand on the wheel, cigarette dangling, Hank Williams pouring through the speaker, the slap slap slap of tar strips on the concrete road, knife of acid stench coming off the low hog barn, there, below the haystack, a muddy chunk flowing up against the meadow weeping green down to the creek that barely flows, those snappers on the log, carp jumps, the close air and in the shadows of the woods mosquitoes hum with desire.

On the ride across the center of the country I fell into the dreams. My cousin and his woman are just starting out, all is fresh, the bad war vanishes into the mists. She is fresh from a mild girl gang in the city where they all sport the same windbreakers with the club name on the back and wear jeans so tight they ache with appetite.

Later, long after the ride, the driver gambles and gambles and one morning in Vegas he has lost it all. He buys a lot sight unseen in some scheme of a desert subdivision and when the payments finally end he owns something worth close to nothing. She becomes a waitress and stuffs the tip money in couches around the house. The children come. The gambling continues, the drinking grows and grows. One night he staggers to the bathroom and vomits violently and comes out blaming the onions in the dish at dinner. The marriage finally ends after a batch of boys and endless debts. The quips never end. He does not complain. He is in his seventies and pencils a letter. He lives in a boarding house on a tiny pension and some pots won at poker. The note has no complaints.

He never stops going on that drive, Hank Williams on the radio, the clean scent of his woman, the glow of the cigarette in the night and next time down at the alley he will roll that three hundred game and then go pro and make a real living and life will be an endless series of strikes.

The car rolls into an old farmstead in Nebraska near the Missouri, the house a small two-story white clapboard, the barn also small. The man comes out in overalls. He is the uncle of the girl with the clean scent and now he looks over her beau. He has black hair, and so does she. He's stooped but still has hard flesh. Chickens cluck and the yard is coarse mown grass, a farmer's yard. There are not flowers, the wife, she's been dead some years.

In the house, he has the table set and the oilcloth has a red and white checked pattern. The plates don't match, the glasses are old jelly jars. He's made sandwiches from a roast he's been sawing on for days. The driver keeps making quips, the old man responds with a faint smile. The girl looks with hope for his approval. Against the wall is an old hoosier with the built-in bin for flour, the sifter and the porcelain shelf that pulls out for the kneading of dough or the moments for rolling out the pie crust for that Sunday dinner. A big pendulum clock ticks, probably salvaged from one of the dying one-room schools. Next to it a crucifix glows on the robin's-egg-blue wall.

The man goes to a cabinet and gets a jar with yellow sauce. Ketchup. He makes his own with low-acid tomatoes. The stomach, you know.

We sit.

I reach for the sandwich and feel eyes.

The old man says grace.

He asks in a soft voice of the city and just what does the driver do for work and is it good and promising. The girl glows, everything will be fine forever and forever. One old milk cow lows near the barn. He keeps it both for the milk and butter. Sometimes he makes cheese also.

I can hear flies buzzing against the screen door leading to the barnyard under the crush of the blue sky. In the cities, the sky is a slit between houses, a fugitive among the trees. Here it is endless and at first too much and then suddenly never enough.

After lunch, he leads us out into the yard. An old weathered door lies on the ground framed by concrete. The old man lifts it up, the hinges creak, dark stairs come in view. Everyone hunches over on the descent. The storm cellar is cool, the walls lined with preserves all yellow and green and red, the relics of last summer's garden. The old man is quiet but almost glowing in the half-light.

We climb back into the yard, goodbyes are said.

As the car rolls down the gravel lane to the road, the driver lights that first desperate cigarette with one-handed ease. He's on the road to the marriage, children, the bets, the bottles, a long highway lined with magic and warm scents and skid marks from the moments he revs the engine and flies off into the ditches.

For the rest of my life I remember the road and that night when life purred across Iowa. The way to the beauty part begins that night on that Iowa road, the voice of Hank Williams, the clean smell of the woman, the soft night air of summer, and all this leads for me to the black metal door and the people lying in darkness and lost to our minds but in some place I sense I once knew, maybe caught a glimpse of the night on the black highway.

There can be no beauty without accepting the people behind the black metal door. Just as I long ago learned that there can be no justice without heeding the man who wants to know which way is Atlanta. And there can be no peace without cranes in the sky and dancing in the marshes.

The Garden

In the asylum, the man who seeks to return to the nation of north is in the room trying to remember the dates of his prison stretches and the charges he faced and my God he can barely bring it back. In part because of the drugs and alcohol but mainly because it lacks texture, it is smooth, an endless road of ruin and mayhem and hangovers and violence and crimes and punishment and one day is like another and the features that cling to the records—the assault, the robbery, the attempted murder—have long been erased from his mind. And he has gathered stubs of bills, old letters with dates, all in an effort to assemble an order to his past that he never experienced.

I walk in the desert. The mesquite stands three or four feet high in the dunes. The people of the asylum are up and some carry large plastic slop buckets out into the sands to be dumped. The dogs have come in from a night of hunting and warring with coyotes and now mill around the kitchen door where men take turns at the table shoveling in menudo. A garden is emerging with columns, plants and shrubs. A waterfall awaits a pump. Behind the black metal door they continue to float in the freedom of their mangled minds. On the wall, paper cutouts shout praise of Mother's Day. A rooster crows, goats call out from their pens. The desert is carpeted with yellow flowers, broken bottles, stacks of tires. The wind is down, a black dog follows me into the sands and keeps its distance as it stalks my wandering. I hit a patch of broken blue tiles, a fragment of a plate, the small tire off a child's toy, the speedometer that has stopped recording motion. A barn swallow sweeps overhead, an orange-crested warbler darts in the creosote. A sign in Spanish stares up at my feet. WHAT TO DO IN CASE OF FIRE, One, Stay Calm.

I can hear chickens clucking, and then a radio blares out *corridos* against the morning calm. Five clotheslines hold the washed blankets of the people of the asylum. A crazy man stands in front of me. He slowly moves a pebble with his heavy army boots, and then, the task completed, he shuffles past me without a glance. In the courtyard, the dogs wag their tails at me. Geraniums bloom in the pot.

There will never be beauty for me unless it comes from the cast-off objects, the broken minds, the buzz of flies, and the roll of dunes where the slop buckets are emptied on a Sunday morning.

The man leans again on the table. He returns to drawing a garden, this time for the insane who are not behind the black metal door but the others, the ones who mill around in the yard, stare off into space and have come here because others say they have lost their minds. The garden he is building, the one with the fountain cascading water, the Roman columns, the trees, potted plants, concrete plaques of lions everywhere, he is calling it the Plaza de los Leones. There will be a band shell also, he is going to build this just on the western edge. Here he will preach and people will sing, guitars will strike up music, bands will blast out under the blue sky. The plaza itself will have a guy just on the southern edge shining shoes, he knows just the man, a compulsive in the asylum. There will be an ice cream cart, the man calling out and peddling helados de Michoacan. He has had this dream so long, a theater of life for the insane where they can promenade, eat ice cream, sit in the shade, listen to music, have their shoes polished.

He draws the scene without pause, the pen flying across the paper.

I ask about the walled compound a mile to the south. In my walk in the shade, I come up on it, the black dog gliding off to the side and almost hunting as I vanish into the dunes. I tell him I could feel something there, something evil. I could not explain this feeling. But I was certain.

He asks, "Did you go in?"

I said, "No."

"Do you remember that photograph I showed you of the dog with the severed human arm?"

About two months before, he continues, just when winter gave way to spring, cars came into the dunes, cars of the state police. He got on the roof with others to watch. The cars went to the compound. Years before the place had been built to warehouse plastic for recycling. But that ended. For twenty or thirty minutes they could hear screams from the compound knife across the sands. Then there were bursts of shots. In the morning, the dog brought the arm.

No, they have not gone out there since.

Did I see any spent cartridges?

The way to the beauty part will not be pretty.

I walk into the sands.

The road is open.

There is this time.

The people smell and stare and make sounds that are not words. They get dirty, hurt each other, explode with anger. When the man who can't remember his prisons arrived here, he was on a stretcher and he was dying. The needle had taken his soul and now was colonizing most of his body. He went into a cell and had to wear a diaper. Just as the people behind the black metal door wallow in shit, so he entered this place like a baby and rather than die, he became someone new made out of someone very old.

There is a crew come to film him for a news show. He is tending the ears of the crazy people, swabbing them tenderly.

The voice asks if he is one of them, one of the lunatics.

He says, “Yes, I am one of them.”

At night the coyotes howl. Sometimes the dog brings in a fresh chunk of a human being.

The man leans on the table, he wants to take people out of the room behind the black metal door and into the light.

Vincent van Gogh

In 1889, Vincent van Gogh vanishes into the asylum after threatening Paul Gauguin with a razor and then slashing the lobe of his own ear and giving it to a woman at a brothel. He continues to paint what others had failed to see. In July he is outside the grounds working, "for days my mind has been wandering wildly, . . . and it must be expected that the attacks will recur in the future. It is frightful. . . . I apparently pick up dirt from the ground and eat it." His throat also hurts from drinking turpentine and from paint in his mouth.

Van Gogh sees the world and in his season at the asylum he paints *The Reaper*, a man mowing down the golden grass of harvest under a pale sun. He sees the work clearly, "it's an image of death as the great book of nature sees it. . . . I find it odd that I saw it like that through the iron bars of a cell." He can feel the attraction of suicide but explains he is like a man who jumps in the river to drown but then finds the water too cold.

The Garden

The man falls into the hole called love. He lives in the crazy place but he is in the yard where sun warms the heart and he is innocent of the life behind the black metal door. He paints a cabin in the mountains and the woods are dark and he says the house is his dream. He is twenty-three, she is nineteen and lives in the city itself in another asylum. And then she kills herself and he paints her as a black silhouette, long hair trailing down her body, and this form of a woman faces a sea of blue—water? Sky? Blue, just blue—and that is all he can say about vanishing into a hole.

There is another man who falls into love and she comes and goes from the asylum. When she is there, she is the woman of his dreams. When she is gone, she sells her body downtown and then he becomes a statue and he cannot move or open his mouth, he paints a man who seems to be screaming and his mouth is either two rows of teeth or a set of bars like those of the cells in the asylum and these bars block entry to the world and then, at those moments, he must be force-fed because he has vanished into a hole. There was a time he was in a drug gang. He came from a family that was half with God and half in the life. He went into the life. He helped hang people, he blew a man apart with a shotgun. There was the military guy they all held down while they chopped off arms, legs and the head with machetes. Then rivals tortured him and he fell silent as he vanished into that hole.

There is a man who killed and killed and then went mad and came to this crazy place. Now he hears the voices in his head and in the dark he talks to Death. He paints men coming with AKs. He vanishes into a hole and screams as he paints.

There is a man who falls in love with a rich woman and lives in the hills over a great city by the big ocean. Then he has suspicions, has machines secretly record her conversations. He decides to kill her and her lover and then himself. He says he cannot live without her. He never does this. The money and the life continue. He falls into a hole but it does not vanish him to some other place. This is not possible once he decides he can live without love.

The beauty part is not a thought.

Early, before the insanity, before the asylum, before the suicide, van Gogh sees something out there on the heath smeared under the gray sky of Holland. He has not yet seen the southern light, he has yet to sense the explosion in a sunflower, the swirl of the stars at night, the fury in the gray-green leaves of the olive trees.

He begins simply: "And then, when dusk fell, imagine the silence, the peace!

"Imagine then a short avenue of tall poplars with autumn leaves, imagine a wide muddy road, all black mud, with heath stretching to infinity on the right, heath stretching to infinity on the left. . . ."

And there are small huts made of turf, the red glow of fires out the tiny windows, puddles of yellow water, the blue sky, trees rotting into peat, all this "and in that sea of mud a shaggy figure—the shepherd—and a mass of oval shapes, half wool, half mud, jostling one another, pushing one another out of the way—the flock."

And there is a farm, a sheepfold, piles of straw, trees, peat, there, at the mouth of the pen, "the door stands open like a dark cave" and "the whole caravan, masses of wool and mud, disappears into the cave—the shepherd and a little woman with a lantern shut the door behind them."

The garden is ready.

There is a time when the snows are deep, the barns collapse, pipes burst, trees crack in the cold. The abandoned graveyards in the forest with the dead from the revolution begin to quake as the old bones seek to flee the ice age that has come. I fall through the ice of a January beaver pond and watch the sky vanish as I sink beneath the waters. That is at the beginning when blue and green smear my dreams and my dreams are of a farm and vanishing into it. When I look at the black metal door and think of the people behind it, that early image of the garden, the blue sky staring at me through the green leaves, that is the garden. But then came all the holes and I fell through them and the garden lingers but it is a memory. The turbulence has taken to other ground and waters.

The music flows and feelings become thoughts and the thoughts are felt, not said, but when you go for the beauty part and vanish through that hole the words stay behind and you tumble with feeling and cannot say what you finally truly know.

There are reports from the vast deep of life, from the regions where my mind roams but my body never visits. In the salmon pens where captives are farmed for market, a new menace arrives. The salmon by nature swim in one direction, a habit that forms mandalas in the sea when they are wild and creates a vortex in their slave pens, a sucking motion that draws the water toward them in the same way a human gated community draws thieves. The jellyfish, drifters all, are sucked up against the pens, the mucus and stinging cells flow into the vortex created by the salmon, the gills are clogged, the fish suffocate and this drives them into a frenzy of motion, the vortex grows stronger, the suffocation accelerates. And the salmon vanish into a hole in the ocean.

The man who had the nightmare about the people trapped behind the black metal door, the people who eat their own shit, he commences building, a wall, a fountain, plants, a place where they can find peace, a place fit for them to leave this world and go to the next.

But the nightmares continue. Two of his assistants in the asylum take turns sleeping on the floor by his bed to comfort him when the night frights become overwhelming.

The crazed soon will punch through the wall and leave behind the black metal door, lie on benches in the sun near the big road where the trucks roar. And vanish into the new garden with water and soothing music. They will tell us nothing. We are on our own.

Vincent van Gogh's father preached around the image of the sower, the man casting seed on the land so that the harvest may come. Vincent repeatedly painted one image over and over, *The Sower* by Jean Millet, a devotee of capturing the peasants of the fields. In those last moments, when he is in the asylum madly painting almost a canvas a day, *The Sower* returns, now a swirl of yellow and blue paint, the sun roaring gold at the world as a man tosses seed into the cauldron of van Gogh's canvas, the day will come when history is clearly seen as an error, the cranes sound overhead, the black metal door swings open and the minds ravaged by life reel into the light of day and face down our world as it crumbles into dust.

The man leans forward on the table. He has taught himself to paint and this passion has taken over parts of his life to his surprise and delight and maybe to his horror. He is a man of God and he understands becoming nothing in prayer, an erasure of his being when drunk with divine grace. But now there is this other thing, when he turns away from the crazy people under his care, when he abandons for the moment his family and his constant need to provide food for over a hundred helpless people, when he stops worrying about bills and threats on his life. When he ceases to be a minister of God or the caretaker of helpless human beings, the sole support for a legion of lunatics. He stares down at the tabletop. He is eating a salad against his will—that artery almost exploded and killed him a year ago and now he must take care or he will not be able to take care of anyone.

He returns to the passion, how he feels late at night when he paints an angel that is full-breasted and naked and beautiful embracing Satan because he knows that only through God can anyone be saved—he is distressed over my willing damnation—and that no one can be written off, not even Satan, that no one is beyond the pale or can be turned away. So he paints, a swirl of colors and they are violent, colors roaring off the canvas. The people in the nation to the north are repelled by his paintings. The people in the nation to the south are drawn to them but have no money for such things.

He says, "When I am painting there in the night, I vanish, disappear. There is no I, no me, just this thing being born and I am not sure what it is, I feel hardly there as it grows from the brush, I . . ." and then he falls away.

Because he has lost that sense of self and yet knows no other way to talk.

That is the beauty part, though he does not say that.

And that is part of the beauty.

Of course, they are crazy, the cranes are just birds and belong to some forgotten past, van Gogh was crazy and died for his art and is on coffee cups and appreciated and of no concern to the rest of us and the hole in the sky is a fantasy, the cranes never vanish, they just come and go, that is their way, the way of beasts.

The garden will soon be finished, the people move out to lie on slabs, the sun overhead, blue sky, the roar of trucks on the highway singing along with the gurgle of water from the fountain, the serene music piped in to ease the souls, the cranes fly overhead, that slow wing beat, and the beauty will be as always all around and invisible to the anxious eye.

The river runs cold, snow in the air, cranes feeding in the fields and the trees tremble with the spring flow of sap, goldfinches and warblers worry the brush and I feel alive, more alive than I ever feel with people, more alive than I ever feel when alone, and I have learned only one thing, never to question why I feel more alive on the river with cold water and the wind brushing against my face coming off the wings of cranes.

And I will leave a hole in my life and vanish seeking the beauty part.

I look up.

A crane vanishes.

Through a hole.

In the sky.

Notes

5 *When I was fifteen*: Brian Moynahan, *Rasputin: The Saint Who Sinned* (New York: Random House, 1997).

5 *Nijinsky is horrified*: Ibid.

7 *If we let ourselves be guided*: Sam H. Shirakawa, *The Devil's Music Master: The Controversial Life and Career of Wilhelm Furtwängler* (New York: Oxford University Press, 1992), 116.

19 *And this woman in the long ago*: Anne Applebaum, *Iron Curtain: The Crushing of Eastern Europe, 1944–1956* (New York: Doubleday, 2012), 140.

72 *The masonry is wondrous*: Annales Franorum, written in 856 AD. The text recounts "a sudden darkness that overtook a small church. A hellhound, with glowing red eyes, was seen as if it was searching for something before quickly disappearing."

80 *He had no more conscience*: Hugh Thomas, *Conquest: Montezuma, Cortés, and the Fall of Old Mexico* (New York: Simon & Schuster, 2005), 77, 80, 152, 156.

80 *He plants the first wheat*: Thomas, *Conquest*, 152.

80 *But when they arrive*: Thomas, *Conquest*, 41.

82 *The slaves are returned*: Thomas, *Conquest*, 205-209.

92 *She parades, she moves lasciviously*: Thomas, *Conquest*, 291.

119–120 *Later, as a young man* (and all subsequent quotations on pages 119–120): Steven Naifeh and Gregory White Smith, *Van Gogh: The Life* (New York: Random House, 2011).

127 *Well, that's how it is*: Vincent van Gogh to Theo, July 1880, Naifeh and Smith, *Van Gogh*.

134 *Why, I ask myself*: Naifeh and Smith, *Van Gogh*.

136 *Our ability to perceive quality*: Aldo Leopold, *A Sand County Almanac, and Sketches Here and There* (New York: Oxford University Press, 1949).

137–138 *Asks a woman in Black*: (and all subsequent quotations on pages 137–138 unless noted otherwise): Naifeh and Smith, *Van Gogh*.

138 *The landscape*: Vincent van Gogh to Theo, October 1884, Naifeh and Smith, *Van Gogh*.

145 *I have the thing in my head*: Naifeh and Smith, *Van Gogh*, 648.

145 *The town disappears*: Naifeh and Smith, *Van Gogh*, 649.

145 *Under the great starlit*: Vincent Van Gogh, *The Complete Letters of Vincent Van Gogh*, Volume Three (Boston: New York Graphic Society, 1981), 445.

150 *I feel more and more*: Letter from Vincent van Gogh to Theo, May 26, 1888, Naifeh and Smith, *Van Gogh*.

152 *Life itself, too*: Vincent van Gogh to Theo, October 1884, Naifeh and Smith, *Van Gogh*.

153 *I am caged*: Vincent van Gogh to Theo, July 1880, Naifeh and Smith, *Van Gogh*.

154 *Anything complete and perfect*: Vincent van Gogh to Emile Bernard, c. July 23, 1888, Naifeh and Smith, *Van Gogh*.

154 *I've done a garden* (and all subsequent quotations on page 155): Vincent van Gogh to his sister Wil, July 31, 1888, Naifeh and Smith, *Van Gogh*.

155 *There are moments in between* (and all subsequent quotations on page 155): Vincent van Gogh, *The Letters of Vincent Van Gogh* (New York: Constable & Robinson, 2011).

158 *I have always had coarse*: Vincent van Gogh to Paul Gauguin, October 3, 1888, Naifeh and Smith, *Van Gogh*.

172 *For days my mind*: Vincent van Gogh to Theo, August 22, 1889, Naifeh and Smith, *Van Gogh*.

172 *It's an image of death*: Vincent van Gogh to Theo, September 5 or 6, 1889, Naifeh and Smith, *Van Gogh*.

174–175 *The door stands open*: Vincent van Gogh to Theo, November 16, 1883, Naifeh and Smith, *Van Gogh*.

ABOUT THE AUTHOR

Author of many acclaimed books about the American Southwest and US-Mexico border issues, Charles Bowden (1945–2014) was a contributing editor for *GQ*, *Harper's*, *Esquire*, and *Mother Jones* and also wrote for the *New York Times Book Review*, *High Country News*, and *Aperture*. His honors included a PEN First Amendment Award, the Lannan Literary Award for Nonfiction, and the Sidney Hillman Award for outstanding journalism that fosters social and economic justice.

ABOUT THE AUTHOR OF THE FOREWORD

Alfredo Corchado is the Mexico Border correspondent for the *Dallas Morning News* and author of *Midnight in Mexico* and *Homelands*.